VISITING SMALL-TOWN FLORIDA

THIRD EDITION

Bruce Hunt

Pineapple Press, Inc.
Sarasota, Florida

For Rudi

Inquiries should be addressed to:
Pineapple Press, Inc.
P.O. Box 3889
Sarasota, Florida 34230

www.pineapplepress.com

Library of Congress Cataloging-in-Publication Data
Hunt, Bruce, 1957-
Visiting small-town Florida / Bruce Hunt. -- 3rd ed.
        p. cm.
Includes index.
IS BN 978-1-56164-488-9 (pb : alk. paper)
1. Florida--Guidebooks. 2. Cities and towns--Florida--Guidebooks. 3. Florida--History, Local. I. Title.
F309.3.H86 2011
917.5904'64--dc22   2011003918

ISBN 978-1-56164-603-6 (e-book)

Third Edition
10 9 8 7 6 5 4 3 2

Printed in the United States of America

CONTENTS

NORTH REGION

CENTRAL REGION

SOUTH REGION

ACKNOWLEDGMENTS

Thank you to June and David Cussen, Shé Hicks, Heather Waters, and Bonnie Nickel at Pineapple Press for their commitment to and enthusiasm for my books. Thanks also to all the Florida small-town residents who have been most helpful and supportive in my research over the years.

INTRODUCTION

*J*UST TO ALLAY ANY CONFUSION, yes, this is my fourth *Visiting Small-Town Florida* book. The first two featured different towns, and therefore were Volumes 1 and 2 of the first edition. That would make the 2003 "Revised Edition" the second, and this one the third edition.

My working title for the original 1997 edition of *Visiting Small-Town Florida* was *Where's Waldo, Florida?* Wisely, Pineapple Press suggested I change that. The "Where's Waldo?" game was popular then, though it is just a footnote now. Of course, I didn't have any idea that fifteen years later I would have a third edition. But I'll go ahead and answer the question. Waldo is about fifteen miles northeast of Gainesville, and is the first in a line of three towns (including Starke and Lawtey) along Highway 301 that have achieved national notoriety as speed traps. When I write *Small Towns in Florida to Avoid*, these will be the first on my list.

At the outset let me say that not all of the places in this book will meet the traditional definition of a town. Some are just a bend in the road with a general store, like Evinston, or just an old irrigation pump shed turned into a tiny post office, like Ochopee. But all have their inimitable charm and merit a visit, even if it's just to pass by. So, interspersed among the chapters on actual small towns, you'll find a few vignettes of even smaller places that I found interesting enough to write about, like Briny Breezes, Stiltsville, and Two Egg—some quirky, some historical, some just remnants of a place now gone.

Back to the criteria for inclusion in this book. As mentioned, there was a "no speed traps" rule. I also had to keep population in mind. In previous editions I adhered to a strict population limit of 10,000, and sometimes that meant eliminating a town I really liked. The best example would be Fernandina Beach, which slipped over the limit to 10,549 in the 2000 census. But Fernandina is an exemplary Florida small town with its successful and ongoing historic-district restoration program, great restaurants, bed & breakfasts, shops, and a scenic setting. I decided that it just wasn't right to leave it out, so mostly for the sake of Fernandina, I relaxed the rule to include towns with populations up to "around 10,000." [1]

Other criteria: Remoteness from or distinctiveness from large metropolitan areas. Remote, like Chokoloskee, at the edge of the Ten Thousand Islands; distinct, like Cortez, which maintains its genuine old-fishing-village character despite metropolitan encroachment. For me the essence of good travel is going to a place that differs significantly from the place where you live. "Visiting" is the first word in my title because this book is meant to be a guide for people who live in larger cities (like me) but crave a change of pace and want to visit someplace different, even if it's just for a weekend or a day. With greater frequency, it seems, the conveniences of the city are being outweighed by its complications—crime, crowding, traffic jams, long lines, and rampant rudeness. Sometimes you just need to get away from all that.

Perhaps the most important thing that I look for is a compelling story in a town's history—sometimes it is trivial, sometimes significant, occasionally it is humorous. Sometimes that history is fairly recent, like Seaside's or Briny Breezes'. Sometimes it is old, like Cedar Key's or Apalachicola's. Among my favorites are towns that have embraced their heritage and devoted time and resources to restoring historic structures and districts—Apalachicola, Everglades City, DeFuniak Springs, Fernandina, and Mount Dora are just a few examples. Doing book research over the years has fueled my interest in Florida history, and consequently each successive edition has had more historical content. I'll confess—I was not a history buff in my younger years. This is a curiosity that came to me later in life. Now, for me, to know a place's story—its history—and then to actually go there and stand on the spot where that story originated is a big part of the magic of travel.

Readers of my previous editions also know well that I have a

---

[1] Please note: Population figures are based on the most recent U.S. Census data, or if not available, the author's best estimate.

soft spot (or perhaps a large spot in my stomach) for local cuisine served up by Mom-and-Pop diners and hole-in-the-wall bar-and-grills, and I've told you about some winners–Wheeler's Café in Arcadia, H & F in Jasper, the Yearling in Cross Creek, The Rod & Reel on Anna Maria. Sadly, a couple of my old favorite places are now gone. Storm surge from Hurricane Dennis in 2005 flooded St. Marks and destroyed Posey's Oyster Bar–a Florida Panhandle icon since 1929. Manny & Isa's Kitchen opened in Islamorada back in 1965, but is now closed. Manny Ortiz and his wife Isa had their own Key lime grove and made the best homemade Key lime pie in the world. I'm going to miss that pie every time I drive down through the Keys. I've found some new spots, though: Eddy Teach's on St. George Island, Star Fish Market in Cortez, Bert's Bar & Grill in Matlacha, Alabama Jack's in Card Sound, and Havana Café in Chokoloskee. You won't go hungry visiting these towns.

There are seventy-five towns or places in this edition, five more than in the previous edition. I trimmed a couple off the list, but added a few more new ones. Most get their own chapter but some I've grouped into one chapter because of their proximity. They are organized, roughly from north to south, into three regions. Most are a simple day trip from within their respective regions. In the Appendix you will find all the pertinent contact information–including websites, phone numbers, and addresses–for every diner, bed & breakfast, museum, and antique shop that I mention.

So, which is it? Is this a guide book? Is it a travelogue? Or is it a history book? I hope that it is all three because I think the subjects are inextricably woven.

You will not find raucous night life, rollicking theme park rides, or performing porpoises in these towns. If you are looking for these things, you have picked up the wrong book. What you will find is the quaintness, peacefulness, and sometimes the quirkiness of real Florida, as personified in its small towns. You will also find some of the kindest and most down-to-earth folks on the planet. In small-town Florida they really do smile and wave as you pass on the sidewalk, even when they don't know you.

In my nearly two decades of research I have come to know small-town dwellers as enlightened, hard-working, resourceful, and happy people. Overwhelmingly, I find them engaged in the betterment of their communities, eager to help their neighbors, and welcoming to visitors. They tend to be independent thinkers who are sometimes eccentric, and often creative, but always welcoming. I'm certain they will welcome you as they have me.

NORTH REGION

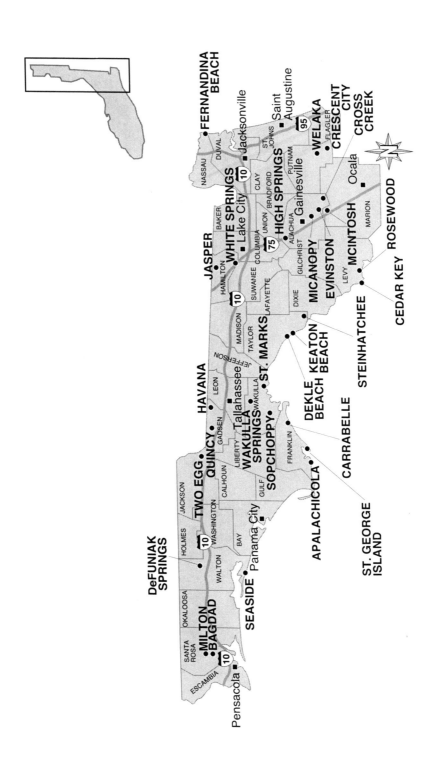

FERNANDINA BEACH

CRESCENT CITY

CROSS CREEK

WELAKA

ROSEWOOD

CEDAR KEY

McINTOSH

EVINSTON

MICANOPY

HIGH SPRINGS

JASPER

WHITE SPRINGS

STEINHATCHEE

KEATON BEACH

DEKLE BEACH

ST. MARKS

HAVANA

QUINCY

TWO EGG

WAKULLA SPRINGS

SOPCHOPPY

CARRABELLE

APALACHICOLA

ST. GEORGE ISLAND

SEASIDE

DeFUNIAK SPRINGS

MILTON

BAGDAD

Saint Augustine

Jacksonville

Ocala

Gainesville

Lake City

Tallahassee

Panama City

Pensacola

Saint Augustine

NASSAU

DUVAL

ST. JOHNS

CLAY

BRADFORD

UNION

ALACHUA

PUTNAM

FLAGLER

MARION

LEVY

GILCHRIST

DIXIE

LAFAYETTE

SUWANEE

COLUMBIA

BAKER

HAMILTON

MADISON

TAYLOR

JEFFERSON

LEON

GADSEN

WAKULLA

LIBERTY

FRANKLIN

GULF

CALHOUN

BAY

JACKSON

WASHINGTON

HOLMES

WALTON

OKALOOSA

SANTA ROSA

ESCAMBIA

95

10

10

75

10

10

10

MILTON, BAGDAD

Population: Milton 8,688; Bagdad 1,490

*P*ine logging and milling in the Milton/Bagdad area trace back to the early 1800s. The two towns, separated only by Pond Creek bayou, grew side by side. Today each has embraced its heritage, and done much to preserve it, making these towns an interesting visit for history buffs.

In 1817 the king of Spain granted land along Pond Creek to Juan de la Rua. De la Rua built and operated a lumber mill there for ten years before becoming discouraged with the local laborers. In 1828, he sold his property to Joseph Forsyth, who took on partners Ezekiel and Andrew Simpson. They built the dam-driven Arcadia Mill, and a village began to grow around it. The vast forests of this region were thick with valuable long-leaf yellow pine, and the Blackwater River provided a ready highway for floating logs down to Pensacola Bay. Forsyth and the Simpsons prospered and took on additional partner Benjamin Thompson. In 1840 they moved the mill a couple of miles downstream to the juncture of Pond Creek and the Blackwater River. A village grew around it again. Joseph Forsyth chose the name Bagdad—perhaps because, like its Middle Eastern namesake, it was wedged between two important rivers. (By the way, that's not a typo. Forsyth spelled it without the "h.")

Bagdad grew up on the south side of Pond Creek, and Milton grew up on the north side. About the same time that Joseph Forsyth and the Simpson brothers were getting the Arcadia Mill into full swing, Benjamin and Margaret Jernigan were starting a mill of their own. People began to refer to the area around it as Jernigan's Landing and also as Scratch Ankle, presumably because of the dense briars that grew along the banks of the Blackwater River. Neither of those names stuck, but a more definitive one, Milltown, did, and it eventually evolved into Milton, which was incorporated in 1844.

More sawmills opened over the following decades. By the turn of the century, Milton and Bagdad had become the most industrialized towns in Florida. The lumber barons thought the bounty was endless, but they were short-sighted. The Great Depression in the 1930s hit both towns hard. Plus, the once-plentiful pine forests had become depleted. The last of the mills, the Bagdad Land & Lumber Company, closed in 1939.

Santa Rosa County Road 191 becomes Forsyth Street as it rolls into Bagdad from the south. On the right, behind a hedge, is the stately pre–Civil War (1847) Thompson House. Arcadia Mill partner Benjamin Thompson built this palatial two-story antebellum mansion with double front porches supported by twelve white columns. During the Civil War, invading Union troops commandeered the house. While there they scrawled a taunting message in charcoal across the parlor wall, which is still there today: "Mr. Thompson, Spurling's First Cavalry camped in your house on the 26th of October, 1864." Originally the house overlooked the Blackwater River, a few blocks to the east, but in 1913 the owners decided to move it in order to make room for their expanding mill operation. They jacked the house up onto log rollers, turned it around 180 degrees, and pulled it by mule to its present location. In 2009 the Thompson House finally got its own Florida Heritage Site designation and State Historical Marker.

Four blocks away, at the corner of Bushnell and Church streets, the Bagdad Village Preservation Association operates the Bagdad Historical Museum in a restored circa-1880s church building that was Bagdad's first African-American church. Displays there tell the story of Bagdad's and the surrounding area's early days and particularly of Bagdad's involvement with the Civil War. During one battle of note that took place here in October, 1864, the aforementioned Union colonel Thomas Spurling and some 200 troops raided a Bagdad logging operation. Confederate troops engaged them in a battle that lasted for two hours.

Across Pond Creek Bridge, Milton has grown into a sizable town, with a population of more than seven thousand. The downtown district has been nicely renovated, particularly Caroline Street (Highway 90) and Willing Street, which parallels the Blackwater River. Downtown reminds me of a miniature Savannah or New Orleans French Quarter. Riverwalk Park—with its pink-blossoming crepe myrtle trees, brick walkways, wrought-iron-and-wood park benches, and gas lamp–style street lights—occupies the waterfront behind Willing Street.

Devastating fires swept through downtown Milton in 1909 and again in 1911, leveling much of the district. But this was boom time, and the town was rebuilt bigger and better than before. Two notable brick buildings—the three-story Imogene Theater on Caroline Street, and the Exchange Hotel at the corner of Caroline and Elmira Streets—were part of Milton's rebirth from the ashes.

Architect Walker Willis designed the theater. It was originally called the Milton Opera House when it opened in 1912. When the Gootch family bought it in 1920, they renamed it after their eleven-year-old daughter, Imogene. A post office and a store shared the first floor. The upstairs theater ran vaudeville shows and silent movies and later "talkies" until it closed in 1946. The Santa Rosa Historical Society restored it in 1987 and turned it into the Milton Opera House Museum of Local History. Unfortunately, fire struck the area again in January 2009, so once again the Historical Society is working on restoration—shooting for a reopen by summer 2011.

1909 Milton Railroad Depot, West Florida Railroad Museum

Charles Sudmall, who operated the local telephone exchange in the early 1900s, was so impressed with the new Milton Opera House that he hired the same contractor, S. F. Fulguhm Company of Pensacola, to build the Exchange Hotel in 1913. Sudmall insisted that the hotel architecturally match the Opera House. The hotel closed around 1946, but it was restored in 1984 and for a while housed the First Judicial State Attorney's Office.

Another restored Milton historical structure, the 1909 Milton railroad depot, sits next to railroad tracks just across the Pond Creek Bridge on County Road 191. Although trains still run on these tracks, they no longer stop here. The original depot, built in 1882, burned in 1907. The 1909 depot was part of the Louisville and Nashville Railroad system. When passenger trains were discontinued in 1973, the depot closed and fell quickly into disrepair. The following year, the Santa Rosa Historical Society formed to save it. The depot reopened on July 4, 1976. It now houses the West Florida Railroad Museum.

Just west of Milton and Bagdad (off Highway 90) you'll find the Arcadia Mill Archeological Site and Museum. Local historian Warren Weekes found the remains of the original mill while canoeing up Pond Creek in 1964, and he spearheaded its archeological excavation.

When I spoke to Warren Weekes in 1998 (he was the museum curator at the time), he told me about Arcadia in the 1840s. "Back then, you were not allowed to acquire property and then turn right around to resell it. When Juan de la Rua got this property from the king of Spain, he had to keep it, improve it, and work it for a minimum of seven years. He paid the king of Spain one shipload of square lumber per year in taxes. When de la Rua sold the property to John Forsyth for four hundred dollars, he was glad to get rid of it. Apparently he was less interested in running a mill and more interested in politics. Later he would become mayor of Pensacola. The Arcadia Mill ran off of two big water wheels driven by Pond Creek. The mill made square lumber with straight saws—the round saw wasn't invented until after 1840. They would cut the long-leaf yellow pine lengthwise, flip it on its side, and then cut it again so that it came out square."

Sadly, Warren Weekes has since passed away, but the work that he began still goes on. The Arcadia Mill Archaeological Site museum has on display a collection of old photographs from the mill's era, as well as artifacts excavated from the Arcadia site by the University of West Florida's Archaeology Department. Students from UWF are still conducting extensive field research and digs there today. From the museum, a trail leads through the woods and down into a ravine, where it crosses a swinging wooden bridge spanning Pond Creek. This was the site of the Arcadia Mill dam and water wheels, re-discovered by Weekes. Beneath the clear water of Pond Creek, you can still see the remains of the foundation of the dam.

DIRECTIONS: From I-10, take Santa Rosa CR 191 north.

DON'T MISS: The West Florida Railroad Museum

DEFUNIAK SPRINGS

Population: 5,122

*L*IKE MANY OF FLORIDA'S HISTORIC SMALL TOWNS, De-
Funiak Springs (established in 1881) began as a railroad stop. But in
this case, the railroad company saw it as more than just a stopover.
Along with rail-line charter rights, the State of Florida had granted
Pensacola and Atlantic (a subsidiary of L & N Railroad) property
ownership covering what today encompasses more than five counties.
The rail line recognized that the area surrounding what is now Lake
DeFuniak and Chipley Park had promise as a scenic community with
recreational offerings. It was a special enough place that they named
it for Frederick DeFuniak, president of the Pensacola and Atlantic
Railroad.

In 1884, the Chautauqua Association chose DeFuniak Springs as its Florida Chautauqua winter assembly location. The Chautauqua Association, based in Lake Chautauqua, New York, promoted a combination of adult education, recreation, and religion. The Florida Chautauqua Association would have a substantial, long-term influence on education and society in DeFuniak Springs.

In 1886, a group of local women in DeFuniak Springs started a library to support the needs of the Florida Chautauqua Association. Renamed the Walton-DeFuniak Library in 1975, it is the oldest continuously operated library in Florida. Located on the inside of Circle Drive, it sits overlooking Lake DeFuniak about a quarter of the way around from downtown. The hardwood-frame building is simply designed with some pleasing exterior motifs typical for that time, such as the diagonal slats on the upper portion of the outside walls and scalloped shingles in the front gable over the entranceway. The original building was completed in 1887 at a cost of only $580. A rear addition was added in 1984 but blends so well architecturally that it appears to have been a part of the original.

1886 Walton-DeFuniak Library

Inside, polished wood floors and large, oval throw rugs give the library a warm feeling. An amazing display of old swords, spears, battle axes, crossbows, and muskets hangs on the walls. The collection originally belonged to Professor Kenneth Bruce from Palmer College in DeFuniak Springs, who left the armaments to the college in his will. When Palmer College closed its doors in the 1930s, the collection was given to the city and later passed on to the library. Many of the weapons are European and date back to the Crusades (AD1100–1300), while some pieces come from Malaysia, Persia, and Japan. The Kentucky muskets date from the mid- to late 1700s.

More historic buildings and homes surround Lake DeFuniak. Just past the library is the 1909 Chautauqua Building, originally the Chautauqua Hall of Brotherhood. Today it houses the Walton County Chamber of Commerce. Circle Drive continues past St. Agatha's Episcopal Church, with its ornate, stained-glass windows. Built in 1896, it is the oldest church on the circle. In the next block, at 219 Circle Drive, you'll find the Bullard House, a three-story, turn-of-the-century Victorian complete with bay windows and a turret with a steeple.

Baldwin Avenue is the main street of DeFuniak Springs' historic district. It runs east and west just across the railroad tracks from Lake DeFuniak. Renovated brick storefronts face south and overlook the lake and the restored L & N train depot, now home to the Walton County Heritage Museum. Chipley Park, on the north side of Lake DeFuniak, has an open-air amphitheater and band shell constructed by the city in 1988, which fits beautifully with the town's turn-of-the-century charm. And it is an idyllic setting for concerts. Many large, pre-turn-of-the-twentieth-century Victorian homes can be found along Circle Drive, which surrounds the almost perfectly round, spring-fed Lake DeFuniak.

Shops and cafés fill the restored buildings on and around Baldwin Avenue. The Book Store, with its large selection of new and used books, anchors the east end. A couple of blocks west is The Big Store in a century-old building that was originally the General Store and Mercantile. It's now filled with antiques and flowers. Around the corner you'll find the Little Big Store—an old-fashion country store. Cross the railroad tracks on Crescent Drive to browse through Dee

South's enormous collection of antique porcelain, crystal, jewelry, and furniture at Southebys Antiques. One room contains nothing but teacups, saucers, and teakettles.

I found two great downtown lunch spots: Murray's Café, on the corner of Sixth and Baldwin (try the fried green tomato sandwich and homemade cakes), and the Busy Bee, a block off Baldwin on Seventh. The Busy Bee has been there since 1916. Although it has had multiple owners through the years, the simple Southern-diner atmosphere and fare have remained constant. The current owner (as of 2009) tells me that there is actually a clause in their property lease that requires that restaurant owners keep the name "Busy Bee."

There is historic lodging here as well. The elegant 1920 Hotel DeFuniak underwent extensive restoration in 1997, and today offers twelve individually themed rooms and suites.

One hundred years ago, DeFuniak Springs was a place that successfully combined Southern small-town charm with sophistication, culture, and education. Today's residents have done (and continue to do) an exceptional job of maintaining that heritage.

DIRECTIONS: Take I-10 to the Highway 331/DeFuniak Springs exit (Exit 85). Go north 3 miles to Highway 90 (Nelson Avenue) and drive another mile west to the downtown historic district.

DON'T MISS: The Walton-DeFuniak Library

TWO EGG

Population: 31

*I*T MAY HAVE BEEN A STRETCH to call two little country stores across the road from each other out in the middle of nowhere a town, but Two Egg had a story that no one could resist. I first stopped into Lawrence Grocery and met Nell King in 1998.

Nell Lawrence King had owned the Lawrence Grocery since 1988. Prior to that, her father, her uncle, and her brothers had all owned it at one time or another.

"I've lived within a couple miles of here all my life," Nell told me. "This is the entire town of Two Egg. Let me count up for a second and I'll tell you what the population is." For about five seconds, Nell mentally ticked off in her head who had had babies lately. "Should be twenty-eight right now. Yeah, we may be a small town, but people do know we're here. The Florida Department of Transportation folks over in Tallahassee tell

Pittman Store

us that the 'Two Egg' ro. sign out on County Road sixty-nine is the most stolen road sign in the whole state."

Of course I had to ask her about the story behind the name Two Egg. It was originally called Allison. Back in the 1890s, a salesman who stopped into the store frequently on his route started calling it Two Egg. Every time he came into the store, he would see the little children of a local farm-working family, the Williamses, bringing in eggs to trade for sodas or candy. It was a large family. Each child had a chicken to care for, and in lieu of an allowance, they could use the eggs from their chickens to barter at the store. The smaller children could just manage one egg in each hand, hence the name.

Lawrence Grocery closed for good in 2007, and in May 2010 the Florida Department of Environmental Protection ordered the demolition of the Pittman Store building across the street in order to dig up an underground storage tank that had not been used since the 1970s. The Pittman Store had been closed since Mr. Pittman retired in 1984. Another piece of small-town Florida history is gone forever.

DIRECTIONS: From I-10 east of Marianna, take Jackson CR 69 north to CR 69A.

QUINCY

Population: 6,765

*H*IGHWAY 12 GLIDES OVER ROLLING HILLS and past oak trees spider-webbed with kudzu on its way into Quincy. It's a reminder that the topography at this northern end of the state blends seamlessly with southern Alabama and southern Georgia. The town of Quincy does the same thing. It is the Gadsden County seat, and consistent with small-town county seats throughout the South, it has a stately dome-topped courthouse with four massive white columns in the middle of the town square. The courthouse has been in continuous use since 1827. A Civil War monument on the south side of the courthouse reads, "Sacred to the memory of the Confederate soldiers from Gadsden County, Florida, who died in the defense of their country."

All of downtown Quincy and most of the surrounding residential area have been designated a National Register Historic District. One of the fifty-five historic structures in the district is the 1912 Bell & Bates Hardware Store Building on North Madison Street, on the east side of the town square. The Bates family still owns the hardware business, and in 1997 they built a modern building on Duval Street behind the original. That same year, they donated the original 1912 building to Gadsden Arts, Incorporated, which restored it and reopened it in 2000 as the Gadsden Art Center, a gallery and educational exhibit center. In 2009 they opened an expansion in the adjacent Fletcher Building, allowing the addition of an artists' co-op and Miss Helen's Espresso Café D'art. At the time of this writing (2010), there were fifteen vernacular art pieces new to the center's permanent collection, including paintings by Thornton Dial Sr. and a "Godzilla" sculpture by O. L. Samuels.

Another historic building of note, round the corner on East Washington Street, is the 1949 Leaf Theatre Building. It was originally a movie theater named in honor of the shade tobacco that was grown in this area for cigar wrappers (see next chapter on Havana). The movie theater closed in 1980. Through private donations and grants, it was restored and reopened in 1983 as a performing arts theater. It has fifteen rows of seats plus a balcony, and its deep-set stage includes a revolving center. Now the Quincy Music Theatre maintains a full schedule of musical productions there.

The surrounding neighborhood is filled with both pre- and post–Civil War homes. A historic walking tour pamphlet, available from the Chamber of Commerce or at the Gadsden Art Center, is the best guide to finding these gems. Two of these historic homes have been turned into bed & breakfasts: the McFarlin House on East King Street, a Queen Anne Victorian built by tobacco planter John McFarlin in 1895, and the Allison House, on North Madison Street, built in 1843 by General A. K. Allison, who would also serve as governor of Florida in 1865.

There is an interesting historical side note that connects Quincy with the Coca-Cola Company. In the early 1900s, patrons of the Quincy State Bank, Florida's first chartered state bank, were told by Mark Munroe, the bank's president, that purchasing stock in a fledgling drink company might prove to be a good investment. Lots of

Leaf Theater

Quincyites took his advice and became very wealthy. For many years, residents in Quincy held more than half of Coca-Cola's outstanding shares. Today they are still thought to own as much as ten percent of Coca-Cola's stock.

DIRECTIONS: From I-10, take the Highway 267 exit #181 and go north.

DON'T MISS: The Gadsden Art Center

HAVANA

Population: 1,677

*B*Y THE EARLY 1970s, tiny Havana had become a boarded-up ghost town. (That's Havana, Florida, twelve miles north of Tallahassee. Locals pronounce it *"Hay*-van-a.") Then, in 1981, Keith Henderson and Lee Hotchkiss, husband and wife antique-shop owners from Tallahassee, came looking for an affordable building where they could relocate their shop. When I interviewed them in 1998, Lee told me, "We originally were just interested in the one corner building, but the owners wanted to sell the whole block and made us such an attractive offer that we bought it all. We talked to all our antique-business friends in Tallahassee about the idea of an antique district in downtown Havana. They loved it, and four of them decided to move their stores here and rent space in the block. We spent

Stained-glass window on H&H Furniture Building

that entire summer and fall renovating. We sandblasted six coats of this awful green paint off the walls. We pulled out the drop ceiling, pulled out all the drywall so that the brick interior walls would show. We put in the wood floors, built cabinets and shelves. It was a chore, and we did it all ourselves. The first weekend we opened up, there were five shops in the block. It was a hit from day one!" Their shop, H & H Antiques, now called H & H Furniture and Design, occupies the bottom floor of the restored 1908 two-story brick building on the northwest corner of Seventh Avenue and Main Street (Highway 27). An old stained-glass window adjacent to the front door depicts a barmaid serving Molly Malone beer. Jasmine ivy grows across the front entrance up to the second floor and around the corner, adding to the historical ambience.

From 1981 on, Havana was a town reborn. A restoration revival began in the downtown district and spread to the surrounding neighborhood. Antique shops, art galleries, and quaint cafés began to open, turning Havana into a destination for visitors from all over the South. Among my favorite Havana shops is Rita Love's Little River General Store, just around the corner from H & H on Main Street. Rita's idea was to open a store that carried nostalgic items—beloved things from our past that we didn't know were still being manufactured. In keeping with the true definition of a general store, she stocks a little bit of everything: food (lots of sauces and spices), an entire counter full of candy, shelves of dry goods, soaps, cookv, kerosene lamps, gardening tools, kitchen utensils, and toys. It seems Rita has traveled through a time machine to acquire the store's inventory. Black licorice, jawbreakers, and bubblegum cigars occupy the candy case. There are even Necco wafers and moon pies, and classic toys like Lincoln Logs, erector sets, and Radio Flyer wagons. The store's brick walls, wood-plank floors, and wood tables and display counters add to the old-fashioned atmosphere.

Next door is another unusual shop, Mirror Image Antiques. They have a tiny art gallery inside a walk-in bank vault, and also a great collection of old baseball cards and old cameras. Most fascinating, however, is their Pete Peterson collection of Oriental antiques. Pete Peterson was the United States ambassador to Vietnam just after the war. Some pieces in the collection date back to the fifteenth century.

Hungry antique shoppers will find ample sustenance at two downtown Havana eateries: Tomato Café and Joanie's Gourmet Market & Fabulous Café.

In the 1990s Keith and Lee took on another project: the mid-1800s McLauchlin House, a large dogwalk–floorplan farmhouse now located one block west of H & H Furniture and Design. It has a wide, shaded wraparound porch with ornate gingerbread trim. When I asked Keith about the house, a smile formed on his face. "That's an interesting story," he told me. "The McLauchlin House was built in the eighteen-forties. It was on a farm about twenty miles north of here in Decatur County, Georgia. One of the residents here in Havana, Nellie McLauchlin Cantey, was born in the house in eighteen-ninety-nine. She also married her husband, Joe Cantey, in the house in nineteen-nineteen. When Nellie's brother passed away, the family considered selling the farm. Lee and I went up there to buy some of the furniture, and we just fell in love with the house. We talked to them about buying it, along with some of the acreage. It turns out that the family really wanted to keep the property, but no one was going to live in the house. Then Nellie came up with a wonderful plan. She offered to give us the house on two conditions: one, that we pay the expense to move the house, and two, that we move it to Havana, where she could be near it. Needless to say, we accepted her offer. The house movers had to cut it into three sections to transport it. In nineteen-ninety-four, not long after we finished fixing it up, Nellie and Joe celebrated their seventy-fifth wedding anniversary in the house."

The people of Havana have done a remarkable job of creating something fresh out of the remains of what was almost lost forever—not just restoring the buildings but reviving the town's heritage too. Havana was originally incorporated in 1906 and named in honor of the Cuban tobacco that had been widely cultivated in this area during the previous three-quarters of a century. In later years, tobacco farmers in Havana specialized in growing "shade tobacco," the leaves of which cigar makers use as the outer wrapper of cigars. They called it shade tobacco because they grew it under cheesecloth tarps, which let just the right amount of light through in order to grow perfect leaves. The harvested leaves were then carefully dried over charcoal-pit fires. The entire operation was a delicate process. In the mid-1960s, under a foreign goodwill program sponsored by the United States government, the north Florida shade tobacco growers' special farming and harvesting techniques were taught to workers in several South American countries. Within just a couple of years, these countries were producing shade tobacco at a significantly lower cost, and the growing industry around Havana (and, consequently, the town itself) died. It would be almost two more decades before Keith Henderson and Lee Hotchkiss would come along and begin CPR on Havana's downtown district.

DIRECTIONS: Travel 12 miles north of Tallahassee on Highway 27.

DON'T MISS: The Little River General Store

FERNANDINA BEACH

Population: 11,636

*A*s I mentioned in my Introduction, in previous editions of *Visiting Small-Town Florida*, one of my criteria for a town's inclusion was that it must have a population of less than 10,000. Fernandina has slipped just over that point, and I'll confess: That is the main reason I relaxed the rule for this edition. That's how much I like Fernandina Beach, on Amelia Island. I think it is one of the best examples of just how successful a renovated historic district can be.

Thirteen-mile-long Amelia Island, just north of Jacksonville, anchors the northeast corner of the state. To reach it from the south you can drive up Highway A1A or cross the St. Johns inlet on the ferry at Mayport. From the north it can be reached by bridge. The very plush Ritz-Carlton Amelia Island Resort, where the world-renowned classic car show Amelia Island Concours d'Elegance takes place each March, sits on the coast in the central part of the island. The town of Fernandina Beach occupies the north end.

Downtown Fernandina Beach received designation as a National Register of Historic Places Historic District in 1973, and that was expanded in 1987 to what today encompasses about fifty blocks. Beginning in 1977 Fernandina's main street from 8th Street down to Front Street underwent an extensive makeover. It was part of Atlantic Avenue at that time, but the city decided that along with its renovation, for the historic section they would revert to the street's original pre-turn-of-the-century name, Centre Street. Now gas lamp–style streetlights stand over brick crosswalks at each intersection, and sidewalks wind around oak trees and benches, making it very pedestrian friendly. Business owners followed suit, renovating their buildings to match the street's new look. Credit for this transformation goes to the Fernandina Restoration Foundation, spearheaded by native resident and attorney Buddy Jacobs. Other Florida small towns have done similar work in more recent years, but Fernandina was one of the first, and the process continues today. When I visited Fernandina in early 2010, I found it bustling even in the middle of an economic downturn: The restaurants were full and the shops were busy. I think they got it right back in the 1970s and they are still getting it right today.

Residential Fernandina is filled with grand 19th-century Victorian mansions—many restored, and some now elegant bed & breakfasts. Great examples can be seen on South 7th Street and on North 6th Street. The Bailey House (once a bed & breakfast, now a private residence) at the northeast corner of Ash and South 7th Street is a beautiful example of Queen Anne architecture. Its two octagonal turrets, one large and one small, extend to the third floor. Some of the windows are stained glass. Completed in 1895, it took steamship company agent Effingham Bailey three years to build. The house remained in the Bailey family until the early 1960s. The C. W. Lewis "Tabby" House, directly across from the Bailey House on South Seventh Street, was built in 1885. Tabby, a poured mixture of oyster shells and cement, was used to build the walls. The rough texture doesn't accept paint well, so it remains in its natural, brownish-gray state.

The mint green Addison House, across from the Tabby House on Ash Street, is another beautifully renovated home. It was built in 1876 by a local merchant. Today it is the luxurious Addison on Amelia Bed & Breakfast. With an addition of two buildings (perfectly matched with the architecture of the original) in 1996, the Addison now has fourteen elegantly appointed rooms with every modern amenity.

Two blocks further south on Seventh Street is the historic Fairbanks House. George Fairbanks was a Confederate Army major who later became editor of Fernandina's *Florida Mirror* newspaper. The house is a colossal three-story Italianate estate. The grounds take up half of the block between Beech and Cedar streets. Fairbanks commissioned famous architect Robert Schuyler to design it, and history books report that he had it built as a surprise for his wife. Apparently Mrs. Fairbanks was not pleasantly surprised, and the house became known as "Fairbanks' Folly." Theresa and Bill Hamilton, owners of the Fairbanks House Bed & Breakfast, are not convinced that is how it really happened.

"Just look at the size of these closets—and the number," Theresa said to me. "Look at the layout of the kitchen. A woman was involved

Fairbanks House Bed & Breakfast

in the design of this house, and I think it's likely that it was Mrs. Fairbanks. The house was built in 1885, at the height of Fernandina's 'Golden Era.' This was the most opulent of quite a few mansions that were being built during that time. My guess is that there might have been some jealousy in the neighborhood when this house was going up. Rumors get started, stories get told."

The Fairbanks House Bed & Breakfast has nine rooms in the main house—one that includes the fifteen-foot-high, third-floor tower, plus three rooms in separate cottages. Most of the rooms have their own fireplaces and Jacuzzi tubs. The Hamiltons supply everything their guests might need, from bicycles to beach chairs and umbrellas. And their gourmet breakfast is always a feast.

There is great lodging on the beach, as well, at the Elizabeth Pointe Lodge, a half-block south of Atlantic Boulevard. Elizabeth Pointe's twenty-room main lodge, with its faded gray shingles, looks like an old Cape Cod mansion, but it was actually built in 1992. The lobby, breakfast room, and sitting room look out over the Atlantic Ocean and are decorated in a nautical motif. The adjacent two-room Miller Cottage and four-room Harris Lodge architecturally match the main lodge.

Great restaurants abound in Fernandina, but each time I visit I save one night for dinner at one of my favorite restaurants anywhere, the Beech Street Grill (at Beech and Eighth streets). A couple other

Elizabeth Pointe Lodge

superb eateries: Joe's 2nd Street Bistro, in a restored 1901 house a block off Centre Street; 29 South—the spot for Sunday brunch; and on my last trip I discovered this marvelous little bakery a half-block north of Centre Street, Patty Cakes Bakery—wonderful cinnamon buns!

A block south of Centre on 3rd Street, you'll find one of Fernandina's most historic structures: the Florida House Inn. It was built in 1857 by the Florida Railroad Company, owned by David Yulee, Florida's first U. S. senator. The Florida Railroad Company built Florida's first cross-state railroad, which ran from Fernandina (construction began in 1856) to Cedar Key (completed in 1861). In the decades following the completion of both the railroad and the hotel, the Florida House Inn was the place to stay. It hosted many dignitaries: President Ulysses S. Grant stayed here, and José Martí—renowned Cuban patriot during the Spanish-American War—was a frequent visitor, not to mention an assortment of Carnegies, DuPonts, and Rockefellers. This was Florida's oldest continuously

Florida House Inn, Fernandina Beach

operated hotel. The inn was closed for most of 2010, but underwent renovation and reopened in December 2010. The Palace Saloon (see the cover photo), at the northwest corner of 2nd and Centre streets, is likely Florida's oldest operating saloon. German immigrant Louis Hirth bought the building and opened the bar in 1903. It had been constructed in 1878 as a haberdashery. Even if you are a teetotaler, you should stop in and see this historic establishment. There were plenty of bars in Fernandina around the turn of the century, but the Palace was considered the "ship captain's bar"—a hangout for the elite. Push open the Old West–style swinging doors and you will step back in time ninety years. It's easy to picture Vanderbilts, Rockefellers, and DuPonts toasting their good fortune alongside sea captains and sailors on shore leave in here. The sixteen-foot-high ceilings are ornately formed from pressed tin—popular in nineteenth-century architecture but a lost art today. In 1905 Hirth added the forty-foot-long, hand-carved mahogany bar with mahogany caryatids supporting the mirror behind the bar. In 1999 a fire burned much of the Palace's interior, but after a two-year restoration, it reopened in 2001. Thankfully, the mahogany bar and its original fixtures were saved.

A stroll down Centre Street could take a while because you will want to stop in every quaint little shop. A few of my favorites are: Celtic Charm, which carries music, books, and hats, all from Ireland; Hunt's Art and Artifacts Gallery; Books Plus; and The Book Loft Bookstore, with a great selection of cookbooks from all over the South.

A couple blocks down Third Street, the Amelia Island Museum of History occupies the old Nassau County Jail House, built in 1878. In 1935 it was remodeled into a brick building, and was an active jail until 1975. The museum took it over in 1986. The museum has a wonderful collection of maps, documents, and artifacts—some that predate recorded history and many from the seventeenth and eighteenth centuries. I found quite a bit of the historical information for this chapter there. Caretakers also conduct guided tours of historical Fernandina and offer specialized field trips—their tour of Amelia Island's cemeteries looks most interesting.

Amelia Island's early history is as rich as any location in the state.

Eight countries' flags have flown over the island (more than any other location in the United States). First the French arrived. Huguenot Jean Ribault was the first European to set foot on Amelia Island (which he named "Isle de Mai") in 1562. This didn't sit well with the Spanish, since Juan Ponce de León had claimed all of Florida for Spain when he landed just north of present-day St. Augustine in 1513. So, in 1565, the Spanish sent Pedro Menéndez de Avilés to kick the French out of Florida and off Isle de Mai, with great success. They renamed the island "Santa Maria."

Later there were invasions from the British—the earliest around 1702—but the island remained a Spanish territory until the first Treaty of Paris ended the Seven Years' War in 1763, and Britain returned Cuba to Spain in exchange for all of Florida. British General James Oglethorpe gave Santa Maria its new name, "Amelia," after the daughter of King George II. But the British underestimated how unfriendly the Indians could be, how much swamp land there was, and how many mosquitoes, snakes, and alligators there were in Florida, so twenty years later England traded Florida back to Spain. In 1812, a small group of U. S. patriots who called themselves the "Patriots of Amelia Island" overthrew the Spanish on the island and raised their own flag for a very brief time. In the summer of 1817, Scottish soldier Sir Gregor MacGregor seized control of Spain's recently completed island fortification, Fort San Carlos. MacGregor flew his "Green Cross" flag, but withdrew a short time later. A few months after that, French pirate Luis Aury raided the island and raised the Mexican flag—unbeknownst to Mexico, by the way. By December of that year, U. S. troops had taken over the island and were holding it in trust for the Spanish. In 1819, Spain and the United States signed a treaty: the U. S. got Florida in exchange for taking over $5 million in debts that Spain owed the citizens of the United States. It took two years to iron out all the details, but in 1821 the United States officially acquired Florida and, consequently, Amelia Island from Spain. In April 1861, Confederate troops occupied Fort Clinch at the north end of the island, but Federal troops regained it a year later.

It was the railroad that turned Fernandina into a thriving place in the mid- and late-nineteenth century. Originally the town was located about three-quarters of a mile north of its present location. In the

1850s, David Yulee promised its residents prosperity if they would agree to move the community south—closer to his railroad terminus and port on the Amelia River. They agreed, and Fernandina's Golden Era began. In a short time, luxury steamers from the North began bringing wealthy vacationers to Amelia Island. Luxury hotels were constructed, both in town and on the beach. Palatial Victorian mansions went up on the streets north and south of Centre Street. Fernandina's naturally deep harbor allowed large ships into its port, and the lumber, cotton, turpentine, phosphate, and naval stores shipping and rail transport industries boomed. The Spanish-American War in 1898 generated even more shipping and rail business. Not only had Yulee kept his promise, but the results of his efforts exceeded everyone's expectations. For nearly fifty years, the new Fernandina was both a world-renowned resort and a center of commerce.

During this time, Standard Oil mogul and railroad tycoon Henry Flagler set his sights on Florida. In the 1880s, he began building resort hotels along Florida's east coast. As they were completed, he would string them together with his railroad. Flagler bypassed Amelia Island, choosing not to connect with Yulee's railroad line. As a result, by the early 1900s, Fernandina's tourist trade had moved south to St. Augustine (to Flagler's Ponce de Leon Hotel) and to West Palm Beach (to Flagler's Royal Poinciana Hotel). Fernandina's flourish fizzled almost as rapidly as it had begun. Had Flagler chosen to bring his rail line through Fernandina, Amelia Island may well have turned into a Manhattan Island South. The Victorian-era homes and Centre Street brick buildings would then, no doubt, have been replaced with larger and more modern structures. In a roundabout way we can probably thank Henry Flagler for his part in saving the Fernandina that exists today.

There's more history to be found at Fort Clinch State Park on the northern tip of the island. The road through the park turns north off Atlantic Boulevard, a few blocks in from the ocean, then winds through a tunnel of myrtle oaks. Thirty-foot-high sand dunes separate the road from the beach. Fort Clinch—named for General Duncan Lamont Clinch, who served during the Second Seminole War (1835–1842)—was built in 1847 (additional construction continued for several decades) by the United States to protect Cumberland Sound. No battles were fought here, but it was occupied by Confederate troops in 1861 and 1862 during the Civil War. Federal troops reoccupied it following General Robert E. Lee's order to withdraw. It was activated again during the Spanish-American War in 1898. Captain J. F. Honeycutt was given its command, but he found the fort half buried in sand and overgrown with cactus and weeds. Worse than that, the fort was infested with rattlesnakes. Honeycutt's crew spent most of their brief tenure restoring the facility to livable and usable condition. The State of Florida bought the fort in 1935 and began restoring it. Its last military occupation came during World War II, when the Coast Guard set up a station here.

Now Fort Clinch appears once again as it did during the Civil War. Park rangers dressed as Union soldiers reenact the daily lives of soldiers garrisoned here in 1864. On one of my visits I found a group of visitors in the infirmary (in the interior compound) who were listening to a Civil War medic describe his duties and his surgical tools. "These are my joint separators," he was saying. "It's much easier to do amputations with these than it is with a saw." I'm not sure I could have stomached medical attention during Civil War times.

The surrounding walls of the five-sided fort are four-and-a-half-foot-thick brick with tabby (concrete and shell) reinforcement. Ramps lead from inside the fort to the tops of the walls. Ten enormous cannons, placed atop the two walls that face the water, guard the sound. From here there is a terrific view across the sound, of shrimping fleets heading out to the Atlantic, and beyond that of Cumberland Island, Georgia.

DIRECTIONS: Go just north of Jacksonville on Highway A1A.

DON'T MISS: The Palace Saloon, the Beech Street Grill

SEASIDE

Population: 300

*W*ALTON COUNTY ROAD 30A detours off of US Highway 98, just east of Destin, to follow twenty miles of coastline along Florida's "Emerald Coast"—a stretch of beach consistently rated among the top five most beautiful beaches in the United States. Its blinding white sand consists of powdered quartz washed down over the eons from the Appalachian Mountains. It squeaks when you walk on it. Low-key beachside communities Blue Mountain Beach, Grayton Beach, and Seagrove Beach have sat nestled here among the sand dunes, sea oats, and wind-stunted scrub oaks, little changed for over half a century, but Seaside sprung up anew in 1982.

Developer Robert Davis grew up in the 1950s in Birmingham, Alabama, but spent his childhood summers on the beach at Seagrove, near eighty acres of undeveloped land that belonged to his grandfa~. In 1978, Davis inherited the property. Three years later he and his wife Daryl built a one-story, tin-roofed, wood-frame beach cottage there that set the tone for what would become Seaside. Inspired by the memories of his childhood summers, Davis envisioned a small beach town with sand-and-shell pathways winding between wood-frame bungalows; a tranquil place where people could enjoy life at a relaxed pace. He went to architects Andres Duany and Elizabeth Plater-Zyberk at Arquitectonica in Miami to help plan the layout and to draw up the town's building code. The first houses went up in 1982, and Seaside evolved into what became the much-heralded model for New Urbanism—a community design concept that attempts to maximize the interaction of neighbors, and to place a town's living quarters within walking distance of its commercial center. The concept is based largely on old (but sound) ideas and on a desire to return to pre–World War II (read: pre–suburban sprawl) neighborhoods and towns. Seaside is an ideal size: You can walk leisurely from one end of it to the other in less than half an hour.

Painted in pastel turquoise, blues, yellows, pinks, and purples, most all of Seaside's homes adhere to a frame-cottage, beach-bungalow vernacular style, with tin roofs and screened porches with gingerbread detailing. But of the three hundred or so houses, no two are alike. Some are tiny one-bedroom getaways; others are five-bedroom family compounds. The walkways, front porches, and small picket-fenced front yards all encourage neighborliness. Upper-floor porches and rooftop gazebos give many of the cottages postcard vistas over top of the town and out over the Gulf of Mexico. They do have numbered street addresses, but everyone knows them by their owner-given names: Take Five, Seaspell, Serendipity, Blue Heaven, Our Place by the Sea, Mis-B-Haven Cottage, Always Five O'clock.

Some of Seaside's residents are year-round, but for most this is their second home. Many of the cottages can be rented through the Seaside Cottage Rental Agency. There's also a terrific bed & breakfast—Inn by the Sea, Vera Bradley—and a vintage 1950s-style nine-room motel called the Seaside Motor Court. Seaside covers the gamut of amenities for its guests. Within its limits are tennis, croquet, and shuffleboard courts; bicycle and sailboat rentals; three

Natchez Pavilion

pools; a fitness center; and a chapel. The town even has its own Seaside Repertory Theatre group, which performs from late March to early October in the Meeting Hall and the Amphitheatre.

While there is plenty to do here if you're feeling active, the most popular Seaside activities tend toward the passive—reading a book on the back porch, strolling along the beach, or bicycling through Seaside's brick back roads and admiring the quaint architecture.

Seaside's focal point, the town square, faces CR 30A, and the eighty-acre town fans out behind it. The square has an amphitheatre for concerts and is surrounded by galleries, restaurants, and, of course, shops. There are two shops in particular on Central Square that should not be missed. The first is Seaside's marvelous (and aromatic) grocery/delicatessen/bakery, The Modica Market, with gourmet goods stacked on fifteen-foot-high shelves that require rolling library ladders to reach their tops. (If you're renting a cottage, you can call ahead and have them stock your refrigerator.). And the second is Sundog Books with its great inventory of mysteries, southern fiction, and other beach books.

Ruskin Place, a block-long European-style plaza, is Seaside's art gallery district, where you will find work by both local and international artists, sculptors, and photographers at Keramikos, Studio 210, and Newbill Collection by the Sea.

Across County Road 30A, on the beach side atop the dunes, is Seaside's open-air marketplace, with beach attire and surf shops as well as a popular walk-up eatery—Pickles (breakfast, burgers, and beer). And then there is Bud & Alley's—named after the owners' dachshund and alley cat—a fixture since Seaside's earliest days. This is Seaside's—and, I think, one of Florida's—finest restaurants. Its menu features a wide assortment of Floribbean, Creole, French, and Italian dishes, plus some that defy categorization. Among the restaurant's many entrées are Basque Seafood Stew with fresh clams, mussels, scallops, and shrimp in a saffron-fennel broth; Florida Blue Crab Cakes on balsamic greens with roasted pecans and lemon butter; and the Bud & Alley's signature dish, Carpet Bag Steak, a wood-grilled tenderloin stuffed with fried Apalachicola oysters, smothered in béarnaise, and served with garlic mashed potatoes.

Nine whimsical open-air pavilions with boardwalks serve as passageways across the dunes and down onto the glorious beach. Each is a unique piece of functioning sculpture designed by a different architect. With airy frameworks, arches, and a hint of Art Deco style, they have become Seaside's icons.

In recent years, Seaside's success has spawned some new developments nearby—Rosemary Beach and Carillon Beach to the east, and Watercolor immediately to the west. While County Road 30A has gained some additional traffic, Seaside's holiday-town charm and magic remain.

A popular 1998 movie *The Truman Show* (starring Jim Carrey) brought some national attention to Seaside. Production designers needed an idyllic small town as a backdrop for the film. They

West Ruskin Street Beach Pavilion, Seaside

considered building a movie-set town from scratch on Paramount's lot until someone showed them a picture of Seaside. In *The Truman Show,* Jim Carrey's character isn't allowed to leave the town. But in the real Seaside you can leave anytime you want to. However, it is unlikely that you will ever want to.

DIRECTIONS: Take Highway 98 west of Panama City to CR 30A. Head south and then west along the shore.

DON'T MISS: Bud & Alley's Restaurant

APALACHICOLA,
ST. GEORGE ISLAND,
CARRABELLE

Population: Apalachicola 2,207; St. George Island 700; Carrabelle 1,231

*I*T MAY BE IN THE MIDDLE of the Florida Panhandle's "Forgotten Coast," but there is nothing forgettable about Apalachicola's great seafood or its picturesque location at the mouth of the Apalachicola River. Rightfully known as the "Oyster Capital" (ninety percent of Florida's oysters come from here), Apalachicola has worked hard to maintain its status as a working town whose livelihood has, for centuries, been tied to the sea. For the last couple decades residents have worked equally hard to preserve the town's history and historic structures, making Apalachicola a magnet for vacationers.

Sometimes visitors fall in love with Apalachicola and just decide to stay. That was the case for Michael Koun, who came in 1983 and bought a dilapidated three-story Victorian hotel in the downtown

Gibson Inn

area called the Gibson Inn—originally the Franklin Inn when James Fulton Buck opened it in 1907. The name changed when sisters Annie and Mary Ellen Gibson bought it in 1923. Michael, with help from his brother Neal, spent two years and over a million dollars meticulously rebuilding and restoring the Gibson Inn to its original turn-of-the-century grandeur. Four-post beds and period antiques fill each of the inn's thirty guest rooms. The downstairs lobby, restaurant, and bar are finished in ornately crafted cypress. Wooden-slat blinds decorate the windows, and rockers and Adirondack chairs sit on the wrap-around verandas. Koun's restoration helped kick off a wave of renovation in downtown Apalachicola and the surrounding residential neighborhood that continues today.

Some of the palatial homes in the neighborhood just west of downtown belonged to wealthy 1900s lumber barons. One—the Coombs House—is now an elegant bed & breakfast. James Coombs, who made his fortune milling and shipping cypress, built the home in 1905. Interior decorator Lynn Wilson, known for her renovation work on historic hotels like The Biltmore in Coral Gables and The Vinoy in St. Petersburg, bought (with husband Bill) the Coombs House from

Coombs House Inn Bed & Breakfast

the Coombs family in 1992. She spent several years rebuilding and restoring it, and has turned it into a Victorian showcase. Much of the interior is built out of lumber from Coombs' own mills—most notably the black cypress paneling and intricately carved oak staircase. In 1998, Lynn and Bill bought and restored the 1911 Dr. Marks House, one block east, bringing their number of guest rooms up to twenty.

The Apalachicola River has always been the town's lifeblood. In the 1820s this was a big cotton shipping port. From the 1860s to 1880s, sponge harvesting was big here—until the industry moved to Tarpon Springs. In the late 1880s cypress, oak, and pine milling and shipping revitalized the town, and in the 1920s it became the center of Florida's booming seafood industry.

Visitors notice right away that the downtown streets are unusually wide. They were built that way back in the cotton-shipping days so that cotton, unloaded from barges at the docks, could be stacked on the streets and compressed before being moved into the warehouses.

Today, shrimp and oyster boats fill the docks along Water Street.

Those wide streets make it easy to park anywhere and walk the entire downtown. On Market Street—downtown Apalachicola's main street—and on avenues C, D, and E you'll find great antique (lots of nautical pieces), art, and gift shops.

The restored red-brick J. E. Grady and Company Building at 76 Water Street was originally built in 1900 to replace a wooden building destroyed by a waterfront fire earlier that year. John Grady operated his ship chandlery business downstairs, and the French government rented office space for its consulate upstairs. Today, the Grady Market—a clothing, art, and antiques store—occupies the downstairs. Upstairs, The Consulate Suites offers four luxury suites to overnight guests.

There are superb restaurants in Apalachicola, and it's no surprise that seafood is prominent on all the menus. The Owl Café, a block from the waterfront on Avenue D, recently expanded its second floor, doubling the seating area. The restaurant first opened in 1908 to serve the dockworkers. Back then the specialty of the house was "whole loaf," a hollowed-out loaf of fresh-baked bread filled with oysters. Today the menu changes daily depending on what's fresh, but expect delectable entrées like Grilled Blue Crab Cakes or Black Grouper Fillet sautéed with artichoke hearts and roast garlic—and save room for Chocolate Mousse Cake with Toffee sauce. Boss Oyster, a casual waterfront restaurant at the south end of Water Street, serves oysters prepared seventeen different ways—eighteen if you include just plain "chilled on the half shell". Tamara Suarez, a former television producer from Caracas, Venezuela, came to Apalachicola in 1998 and opened Tamara's Café Floridita on Avenue E, later moving it to Market Street. Her menu mixes native Venezuelan recipes with Caribbean and Florida dishes. Try the Pecan Crusted Grouper with Jalapeno Sauce or the Paella, and for dessert don't miss her outstanding Torte Tres Leche Cake. The Apalachicola Seafood Grill, a Market Street icon since 1903, has a terrific Grilled Grouper Melt, and the owners also run the Old Time Soda Fountain across the street. Other great eateries: Nola's at the Gibson Inn, which has excellent Crab-Stuffed Grouper Florentine; Chef Eddie's Magnolia Grill on 11th Street, where Chef Eddie Cass serves up sumptuous New Orleans–style

Apalachicola riverfront

dishes like Dolphin Ponchetrain and Snapper Butter Pecan; and another popular seafood place, That Place In Apalach.

A very interesting chapter in Apalachicola's history is chronicled at the John Gorrie State Museum on 6th Street. John Gorrie was a physician who came to Apalachicola in 1833. He became a driving force in the community and served as mayor, postmaster, and city treasurer. He also founded the Trinity Episcopal Church. His most significant contribution, however, was his invention of the ice-making machine.

Dr. Gorrie treated yellow fever victims during the epidemic of 1841. He was convinced that if he could find a way to cool his patients down, they would have a better chance of recovering. In 1842, he began working on a design for a device that would lower the temperature of the air in a room. By 1844, he had constructed a machine that, more or less, cooled air by removing heat through the rapid expansion of gases (the same basic principle used in air conditioners and refrigerators today). An unexpected byproduct of the process was that the machine made sheets of ice. In 1851, Dr. Gorrie received a U.S. patent for his ice-making invention.

The museum chronicles John Gorrie's remarkable life and accomplishments. On display is a replica of his ice machine, built according to the plans in his patent. The sad ending to Dr. Gorrie's tale is that until his death in 1855, he worked hard to market the machine but was completely unsuccessful. He died never knowing the enormous impact his invention would have on the world.

Outstanding cuisine, elegant accommodations, and an historic "old Florida" setting make Apalachicola, on the "Forgotten Coast," a memorable destination.

Just across the bridge and east of Apalachicola is St. George Island, a thirty-mile-long barrier island. Blinding white beaches, sand dunes, sea oats, and stilt houses characterize the scenery. Pristine Julian G. Bruce/St. George Island State Park occupies the eastern tip of the island. Seclusion is the main attraction here. Most visitors rent one of the beach houses by the week or the month. Don't come looking for a lot of excitement or nightlife here. This is more of a sit-in-a-beach-chair-and-read-a-paperback kind of place. Besides peace and quiet, another of St. George's attractions is the dog-friendly beach. After you have worked up an appetite walking Bowzer on the beach, head to Eddy Teach's Raw Bar for fresh-off-the-boat oysters and an ice-cold beer. Jim and Vicki Frost opened their open-air bar and grill in 2006, and then moved a couple blocks down the dirt road to a location with a little more elbow room in 2010.

There is a new landmark on St. George Island that replaces an old historic one. Little St. George Island, just west and separated from the main island by Government Cut Pass, had been home to one of three versions of the Cape St. George Lighthouse since 1833. The last one, built in 1852, took a century and a half of hurricane batterings before finally being deactivated in 1994. Only a year later, in 1995, Hurricane Opal washed out a significant amount of the foundation, leaving the lighthouse precariously tilted to one side. In 2002 the base was rebuilt and the tower righted, but it wasn't long before erosion put it in jeopardy again. In October 2005 it finally gave in and collapsed. A local group of diligent volunteers formed the St. George Lighthouse Association and took on a massive salvage project, saving more than 22,000 bricks to be reused to build a new lighthouse. Using plans for the 1852 original found at the National Archives, the group built an identical lighthouse, largely from salvaged materials, on main St. George Island—where everyone could see it. The new lighthouse opened in December 2008.

The beach at St. George Island

Eddy Teach's Bar & Grill

New St. George Island Lighthouse

If you are in pretty good shape, hike the ninety-two steps to the top for a spectacular view. Putting it on St. George Island was a stroke of genius. It looms on the horizon as visitors cross the bridge, giving the island a magnificent icon. The museum building, right next to the lighthouse—still under construction when I visited at the New Year in 2009—opened in 2010.

A half-hour east of Apalachicola you'll pass through the town of Carrabelle, on an island at the mouth of the Carrabelle River. In the late 1800s, it was a lumber-shipping town with several large sawmills. Now it's a sport and commercial fishing community that can claim the World's Smallest Police Station, a phone booth in the middle of town, alongside Highway 98. In the early 1960s Carrabelle's police department consisted of one outdoor telephone box, but people kept using it for unofficial business. When an old phone booth became available from St. Joe Telephone Company in 1963, the town commandeered it for its police department. For breakfast or lunch try the Carrabelle Junction coffee shop/diner right in the heart of downtown Carrabelle.

World's Smallest Police Station

DIRECTIONS: Carrabelle is 60 miles southwest of Tallahassee on Highway 98/319 on the coast. From Carrabelle, continue west along the coast to Eastpoint. Head south across the toll bridge, Highway G1A/300, to St. George Island. Continue west on Highway 98/319 across the Apalachicola River Bridge into Apalachicola.

DON'T MISS: The Gibson Inn, the St.George Lighthouse

WAKULLA SPRINGS

Population: 200

"*C*ENTURIES OF PASSION pent up in his savage heart!" is the tag line on the movie posters for Universal Studio's 1954 sci-fi/horror classic *The Creature from the Black Lagoon*. Archaeologists, played by Richard Carlson and Julie Adams, discover the prehistoric gill-man/monster, played by Ben Chapman, while on an expedition deep in the Amazon. Filmed mostly underwater in 3-D, the film was a technological, special-effects marvel in its day. Universal chose Wakulla Springs, fifteen miles south of Tallahassee, as the film's location because of its exceptionally clear waters.

Wakulla Springs, part of Edward Ball Wakulla Springs State Park, is the largest and deepest spring in the world. Its waters are so clear that details at the bottom, 185 feet down, are discernible from the surface. It actually has been the site of numerous archaeological excavations. In 1935, divers discovered a complete mastodon skeleton at the bottom of the springs. The reconstructed mastodon now stands in the Museum of Florida History in the R. A. Gray Building at the Capitol in Tallahassee.

The springs had its own recently living prehistoric creature too—although by all accounts it was not a malevolent one. Old Joe was a 650-pound, 11-foot-2-inch alligator that had been seen at the springs since the 1920s. Although he had never shown aggressive behavior, Old Joe was shot and killed by an unknown assailant in August 1966. Scientists estimate that Old Joe may have been close to two hundred years old. Carl Buchheister, then president of the Audubon Society, offered a $5,000 reward for information leading to the arrest of the gunman, but no one was ever charged with killing Old Joe.

All manner of wildlife thrives in the park. In addition to alligators, there are deer, raccoons, and even a few bears living here. Bird watchers can spot a variety of winged creatures, including anhingas, purple gallinules, herons, egrets, ospreys, and long-billed limpkins (called "crying birds" because of their shrieking, almost human cry). On my first visit to the park, when I passed through the entrance gate, the ranger warned me to be cautious if I hiked the trail down to the Sally Ward Spring. "Where you see the red ribbons," she told me, "that marks the area where one of our momma gators is keeping close watch over her new brood of babies. Needless to say, she's being very protective."

Edward Ball was the brother-in-law of Alfred I. DuPont. He was also the executor and trustee of DuPont's sizable estate and trust. Ball built a banking, telephone, railroad, and paper-and-box manufacturing empire out of the DuPont trust. Dupont's estate was worth an estimated $33 million when he died in 1935. Ball had grown that into more than $2 billion by the time he passed away in 1981 at the age of ninety-three.

One of Edward Ball's proudest achievements was the construction of the Wakulla Springs Lodge in 1937. The twenty-seven-room lodge is essentially the same today as it was in the 1930s. Ball insisted that it always continue to reflect that era and also that it never become so exclusive that it would not be affordable to "common folks." Wakulla

Wakulla Springs Lodge

Springs Lodge reminds me of a palatial Spanish hacienda. Cypress beams with hand-painted crests and scenes of Florida cross the ceiling in the lobby. Blue and gold Spanish tiles frame the entranceway. The floors are mauve, red, and gray Tennessee marble tiles in a checkerboard pattern. A giant fireplace, made from native limestone and trimmed in marble, dominates the far wall. In many ways this is Florida's version of the grand western lodges built during the same era.

A long glass case at one end of the lobby contains the stuffed and mounted remains of Old Joe. His plaque reads, "Old Joe's first and only cage." The most interesting room in the lodge is just past Old Joe's case–the soda fountain shop. There is no bar in the Wakulla Springs Lodge. Instead, Ball, who was fond of ginger whips (ice cream, ginger ale, and whipped cream), had a sixty-foot-long solid marble soda fountain counter installed.

Out on the spring, from the top of the twenty-foot-high diving platform, you can look down on bream and bass schooling on the bottom. The water is amazingly clear: it's like looking through glass. It's no wonder that Hollywood came to this location to film Tarzan features and other movies like *Around the World Under the Sea* and

Airport 77, in addition to *The Creature from the Black Lagoon.*

Wakulla Springs State Park is as serene a setting as you could hope to find. Nature trails leading out from the lodge take hikers through hardwood forest and past sinkholes and springs. The lodge also operates glass-bottom boat tours.

DIRECTIONS: Take SR 61 south from Tallahassee and go east on SR 267.

DON'T MISS: Old Joe

ST. MARKS, SOPCHOPPY

Population: St. Marks 326; Sopchoppy 571

*W*HICH CAME FIRST, State Road 363 or Posey's Oyster Bar in St. Marks? I'm not sure, but if the oyster bar predated the highway, which runs straight south from the Capitol for twenty miles before it dead-ends a half-block from the original Posey's location, then my guess is that some shellfish-loving legislators had something to do with the road's construction. Sadly, in 2005 Hurricane Dennis flooded St. Marks and closed Posey's Oyster Bar, a Florida Panhandle icon since 1929. But all is not lost. Next door to Posey's original location you will find the Riverside Café, serving fresh oysters and seafood, and across the street the café's owners have also opened the St. Marks Smokehouse and Oyster Bar. And if you would like to visit for more than a day, quaint lodging is available right in St. Marks at the restored 1923 Sweet Magnolia Inn Bed & Breakfast.

St. Marks sits at the confluence of the Wakulla and St. Marks rivers. The two combined waterways then flow another three miles south into the Gulf of Mexico. This has been a strategic location for lots of different people throughout history. It was an important village for the Apalachee Indians in 1528, when Spanish explorer Pánfilo de Narváez ran into them on his trek toward Mexico. The Apalachees gave him and his men such a scare that they hastily built rafts and took to the sea for the remainder of their journey. (Narváez and most of his crew drowned during violent storms on the Gulf before reaching Mexico.) In the early 1600s, Spanish missionaries built the Mission San Marcos de Apalache (hence the name St. Marks) because they felt it was important to convert the Indians to Christianity. In 1680, Spanish troops thought that the location had strategic military importance and built the wooden Fort San Marcos de Apalache. Over the next two hundred years, the fort was alternately rebuilt and occupied by Spanish, French, British, and eventually American troops, the last in 1819, when General Andrew Jackson seized the fort following the conclusion of the First Seminole War. Some remains of the fort can still be seen at its site just off State Road 363.

The town of St. Marks was incorporated in 1830, and it became an important shipping port. The Tallahassee Railroad Company built one of the state's first railroads to run from Tallahassee to St. Marks in 1837. Mules pulled the cars. Today that route has been converted into the sixteen-mile Tallahassee–St. Marks Historic Trail, a Rails-to-Trails project.

People come to St. Marks mainly to eat oysters and to go fishing, but there is more to see. The St. Marks National Wildlife Refuge, just four miles east (go back up to Highway 98, then take State Road 59 south), is home to a wide variety of coastal woodlands wildlife—everything from anhingas to alligators. The St. Marks Lighthouse, at the south end of State Road 59 in the Wildlife Refuge, was built in 1829. This eighty-foot-tall, stucco-over-brick structure had to be moved back from the encroaching sea in 1841. Confederate troops were stationed here during the Civil War.

It's hard to resist taking a detour up County Road 319, off Highway 98, just to pass through the town of Sopchoppy. The name is likely a mispronunciation of two Creek Indian words that describe the river that flows past the town: *sokhe* and *chapke*, meaning "twisted" and "long." Or, the Creek Indians might have been describing something else—worms. Worms have put Sopchoppy on the map. The variety that breeds in this area's soil is particularly fat and long—a fisherman's dream. The method used to bring them to the surface is called "gruntin." The worm grunter's tools are a wooden stake and a flattened iron paddle. Something amazing happens when a grunter drives a stake into the ground and grinds the iron paddle against it: worms come wriggling out of the ground by the hundreds. The grunting noise that the grinding makes sends a vibration through the ground that makes the little slimy guys crazy. On the second weekend in April, Sopchoppy holds its annual Worm Gruntin Festival and Worm Grunter's Ball. There's lots of good food and live entertainment and they choose a Worm Queen. The highlight, however, is the Worm Gruntin Contest, held to see who can grunt up the most worms in fifteen minutes. In 1972, Charles Kuralt brought worm gruntin to the attention of the outside world, much to the chagrin of locals. Following that publicity, the U. S. Forest Service began requiring a permit and charging fees for gruntin.

Visitors to Sopchoppy will find a Mom-and-Pop grocery store, a hardware store, and a bait-and-tackle shop. There is also a terrific pizza restaurant called Backwoods Pizza & Bistro, located in a restored 1912 pharmacy building, which doubles as a canoe and kayak outfitters shop.

DIRECTIONS: Take SR 363 south from Tallahassee until it ends at St. Marks. From SR 363 head southwest on Highway 98, then west on CR 319 to Sopchoppy.

DON'T MISS: Eating oysters at the Riverside Café

JASPER

Population: 2,061

*M*ost small towns have a gathering place, the kind of place where, if you fail to check in with established regularity, folks begin to wonder if you've taken ill or something: "Old Henry hasn't come in for breakfast in a coupla days. Wonder if he's taken to feeling poorly?" The kind of place where, if you're an out-of-towner who has stopped in while passing through, the regulars will have learned the better part of your life story before you leave—and you'll have learned a good bit of theirs. The H & F Restaurant in the center of downtown Jasper is one of those places. They are open seven days a week, breakfast and lunch only, and they don't bother with a menu; it's all on the buffet.

The ancestors of most of the longtime locals in Jasper—like those in nearly every small north Florida town—were originally from Georgia, Alabama, and South Carolina. The food here reflects that heritage: fried chicken, sausage, roast beef and gravy, turnip greens (with lots of ham hock), yellow squash, fresh pole beans, okra and tomato, butter beans, cornbread dressing (my favorite), and dessert (bread pudding and three kinds of cake: strawberry, pineapple, and coconut).

"H and F stands for Handy and Frana. That's my mom and dad," owner Maureen Riley told me. "They started the place. Been at this same location since nineteen-sixty-eight. Having it all-buffet makes it easier to operate, plus folks can better choose what they want to eat when they're looking right at it. There's a hunting reserve near here, so we get lots of hunters in here during the season from all over north Florida and south Georgia. Then there're the regulars we get in here day in and day out. They're all like family."

DIRECTIONS: Take Hamilton County Road 6 east from I-75.

DON'T MISS: The cornbread dressing at H & F Restaurant

WHITE SPRINGS

Population: 842

*I*N 1935, the Florida state legislature chose Stephen Foster's melody "Old Folks at Home," better known as "Way Down Upon the Suwannee River," as the official state song. Ironically, Foster never once set foot in the state of Florida, much less on the banks of the Suwannee. (It's likely that, except for a single trip to New Orleans, Foster never ventured south of Cincinnati, Ohio.) In his original draft of the song, which was ultimately published in 1851, he had written, "Way down upon the Pee Dee River," but it just didn't ring true for him. (The Pee Dee River is in South Carolina, and he had never been there either.) With the aid of an atlas and the assistance of his brother, Morrison, Stephen tried inserting a variety of river names into his song, including Yazoo. None sounded right until he hit on Suwannee.

White Springs is home to the Stephen Foster Memorial and Folk Culture Center, a 250-acre park and memorial to the songwriter alongside the Suwannee River. It opened in 1950, ninety-nine years after "Way Down Upon the Suwannee River" was first published.

In the 1700s, White Spring was sacred ground to the local Indians. They felt that the spring, which spills into the Suwannee, had special curative powers. Indian warriors wounded in battle were not attacked when they came to the springs to recuperate. After settlers moved here in the early 1800s, word of the water's medicinal properties spread. Eventually, developers built hotels and a posh health resort and spa around the springs. Teddy Roosevelt was a regular visitor.

Today, there are few remaining signs of White Springs' resort days. Of the original dozen hotels, the only one still standing is the 1903 Telford Hotel, a copper-roofed, three-story brick and stone structure in the center of town. In its day, the Telford hosted presidents Taft and Roosevelt, J. P. Morgan, John D. Rockefeller, George Firestone, and Thomas Edison. Today it is a bed & breakfast and restaurant. The White Springs B & B, another bed & breakfast, is in the historic Dr. Ivey Kendrick House. It belonged to local dentist Ivey Kendrick and his wife Myrtle, who built it in 1905 as a boarding house.

Highway 136 crosses a deep gorge carved by the Suwannee River just before rolling into the tiny community of White Springs. Immediately on the left is White Springs' Nature & Heritage Tourism Center, operated by the Florida State Park Service. This is a good source for books and maps, as well as information for kayakers and festival-goers.

Nearby American Canoe Adventures rents and sells kayaks and canoes, and organizes trips on the Suwannee. Increasingly, year-round visitors are enjoying the beauty of the river from the vantage point of a canoe or kayak.

Just up the road is the entrance to the Stephen Foster State Folk Culture Center. Your first stop should be the Stephen Foster Museum, housed in a large Southern plantation house with six giant two-story white columns on its front porch. The north wing has a collection of old, unusual, and ornate pianos. One of the most interesting is an 1875 Steinway duplex scale piano with six tiered rows of keys. Another is a small, upright Frederick Haupt/Leipzig that Stephen Foster had

Suwannee River

played regularly at the home of one of his neighbors in Pittsburgh. Morrison Foster's fold-out office desk and chair sit against one wall. A plaque describes the desk as the one that Morrison and Stephen sat at while studying the atlas for an appropriate river name for "Old Folks at Home." The center hall contains dioramas that portray scenes described in Foster's most popular songs. In the south wing there are more pianos and a ten-foot-tall Howard Chandler Christy painting of Stephen Foster done in 1948.

The centerpiece of the park is the ninety-seven-bell carillon in the top of a two-hundred-foot-tall brick bell tower built in 1958. The bells are of a tubular construction rather than of the more conventional cast type. The carillon plays a program of Stephen Foster tunes on an electronic music roll similar to a player piano's, and sometimes guest carillonneurs play. Across from the bell tower, in the Craft Square, artisans demonstrate their various centuries-old crafting skills like blacksmithing and wood carving.

The Stephen Foster State Folk Culture Center holds special events throughout the year, but the biggest event is the annual three-day Florida Folk Festival, held on the Friday, Saturday, and Sunday preceding Memorial Day. It is one of the oldest (since 1952) and most popular folk music and folk craft festivals in the country.

Near the park entrance, a wooden walkway leads to a scenic overlook on the banks of the Suwannee. The gorge is nearly a hundred feet deep. The river flows past at a fairly good clip. Limestone boulders hold up the bank on this side, and tall cypress trees, thick with moss, lean out over the water.

The name Suwannee has two possible sources. In the 1700s, the river was called the Little San Juan, in acknowledgment of the San Juan De Guacara Mission located on its banks. Local dialect may have corrupted *San Juan* into *San wanee*. The more likely possibility is that the name is derived from the Creek Indian word *suwani,* which means "echo." This makes sense, because the steep walls of the gorge formed by the river do create a good echo.

DIRECTIONS: Take I-75 to the Highway 136/White Springs exit (Exit 439). Go east.

DON'T MISS: Stephen Foster State Folk Culture Center

KEATON BEACH,
DEKLE BEACH

Population: Keaton Beach 300; Dekle Beach 200

*I*N THE VERY EARLY MORNING HOURS of March 13, 1993, the fourth most devastating storm ever to hit the continental United States made landfall on the north end of Florida's Big Bend area. Its strongest winds struck the tiny coastal communities of Dekle Beach and Keaton Beach, where ten people were killed and 150 homes were severely damaged or destroyed (only two houses in Dekle Beach were left unscathed). The total loss for the entire state of Florida would end up at twenty-six lives and more than $500 million in property damage. Over the next couple of days, the storm would continue across the state and all the way up the East Coast, turning into a horrific blizzard. Because the storm hadn't formed as a traditional hurricane does, it wasn't given a name, despite record storm surges and winds well over one hundred miles per hour. Most simply remember it as the "No Name Storm of 1993." Those who experienced it refer to it as "The Storm of the Century."

On the map, Keaton and Dekle beaches appear as two little dots on Taylor County's coast. Just south of Perry, Highway 361 carves a narrow path west and then south through unpopulated pine forest and eventually cypress marsh as it approaches the coast. This is not "coast" in the conventional Florida sense. There are no natural beaches. The woods and wetlands grow right up to the edge of the usually calm waters of the Gulf of Mexico. This area is known as the Nature Coast. A spur road off Highway 361 (Adams Beach Road) dead-ends at the Gulf. You can look both up and down the coast and not see a single sign of human intervention. It is strikingly majestic. This is probably pretty close to what it looked like to the Timucuan Indians, the original inhabitants of this region.

Continuing south on Highway 361 you'll find Dekle Beach, where one fishing pier and several docks occupy the shoreline and three or four dozen homes sit atop towering stilts. It looks like the owners had a contest to see who could build the tallest stilt house. Most of them are thirty or forty feet above the ground.

Keaton Beach is a few more miles south, and a little larger than Dekle Beach. Keaton Beach sits on property originally owned by a sawmill owner and turpentine producer named Captain Brown back in the mid-1800s. Brown liked his bookkeeper, Sam Keaton, so much that he named the little community after him. Keaton Beach has a small marina and Hodges Park on the tiny man-made beach, and the Keaton Beach Hot Dog Stand is right across from the park.

I call the Keaton Beach Hot Dog Stand "the hot dog stand at the edge of the world." It seems such an anomaly, way out here. A giant shark's head hangs outside over its entrance. Inside it's a cozy eatery with picnic tables and benches, where, in addition to hot dogs, you can get burgers, chicken, and fresh seafood. The hot dog stand has been here since the mid-1970s. It was called Ruth's originally. Martha and Bill Hargeshiemer bought it in 1985 when they moved up to Keaton Beach from Plant City. In 2001, Ron Wheeler, a paramedic from Ohio, bought it from the Hargeshiemers. The first time I visited

Hot Dog Stand

Keaton Beach, I spoke to Martha and Bill Hargeshiemer about the 1993 storm.

"Well, we had a roof left," Bill told me, "but that was it."

Martha pulled three photo albums out from under the counter and passed them over to me. "I was here when it hit. Bill was down in Tampa. Around six o'clock on the twelfth (of March 1993), I called the Coast Guard station down at Horseshoe Beach–they are about thirty-five miles south of here, and asked, 'Is it getting bad?' We have a lot of commercial fishermen in this area, so weather is a constant concern. The Coast Guard station tells me, 'Maybe sixty-mile-per-hour winds and two-to-four-foot seas.' Nobody knew what was coming. It hit like a freight train around three-thirty in the morning. We had one-hundred-ten- to one-hundred-twenty-five-mile-per-hour winds. The storm surge brought flood waters eight to ten feet high here. It pushed water inland all the way up to the curve in the road. Houses floated up off their foundations. At Dekle it reached as high as seventeen feet. That's why all their new houses are built up so high. It continued to blow until about eight o'clock in the morning. Rescue crews spent the next two days removing bodies from the tops of trees over in Dekle."

I thumbed through Martha's photo albums, looking at before-and-after photos of houses and buildings and reading newspaper accounts of the havoc dispensed by the storm. Perhaps to change the subject to something lighter, Martha asked if I would sign their guest book. It contained more than three thousand signatures and hometowns. Travelers from as far away as South Africa, Italy, Norway, and Great Britain have signed the book. Former president Jimmy Carter, his family, and his bodyguards all signed it in December 1996 when they stopped in on their way to Steinhatchee for Christmas.

Across the parking lot is Hodges Park on the beach, where a commemorative plaque dedicates the park to the memory of those who died in the storm and to those who survived. Reading the plaque is sobering: It lists the names and ages of the Taylor County residents who died. Four were children. Whole families were wiped out.

Keaton Beach and Dekle Beach have long since rebuilt, but the memory of March 13, 1993, will stay forever with their residents.

DIRECTIONS: Take SR 361 southwest from US Highway 19, south of Perry, to Dekle Beach and then Keaton Beach just south of Dekle.

DON'T MISS: Keaton Beach Hot Dog Stand

STEINHATCHEE

Population: 500

*L*ONGTIME FRIENDS OF MINE, Michael and Leslie Poole, introduced me to the sleepy Big Bend fishing village Steinhatchee. Along with their two sons, Blake and Preston, Michael and Leslie have been making annual scalloping and fishing trips here for many years. Fishing (both sport and commercial), boating, and scalloping on the grass flats of Deadman's Bay at the mouth of the river are Steinhatchee's prime attractions. The town's name is pronounced "*Steen*-hat-chee," by the way. It means "dead man's river" in the Creek language.

The State Road 361 bridge crosses the Steinhatchee River and connects the towns of Steinhatchee and Jena (*Jee*-na). From the top of the bridge, you have a good view of the docks and wooden shacks that line the river's south shore and Riverside Drive. Looking down into the river is like looking into an inky abyss. It's not pollution that makes the water so black; tannic acid naturally leaches into the river from cypress and pine trees growing along the shoreline.

Two miles upriver, up State Road 51, is the Steinhatchee Landing Resort, a nature-conscious village with fifty Old Florida–vernacular-style cottages and homes, along live oak– and magnolia-shaded lanes. The thirty-five-acre property wraps around a bend on the north bank of the Steinhatchee River.

I spent a weekend at Steinhatchee Landing in a two-story, tin-roofed house on a shady lane. All the houses on this lane are named for spices. Mine was the Vanilla, but it was anything but plain. It was decorated in a quaint, country-farmhouse style and furnished with comfortable overstuffed chairs and couches. It had upstairs and downstairs screened porches with wicker rocking chairs. This is the best of both worlds: Old Florida, Cracker-style architecture built brand new with all the modern conveniences. Most of the cottages are privately owned and all are rented through the Steinhatchee Landing office. Some allow small dogs.

Developers Dean and Loretta Fowler, originally from Georgia, began building this village in 1990. Dean first came down to Taylor County, Florida, in the late 1980s for a weekend fishing expedition at the invitation of a group of banker friends. In his gentle Georgia accent, Dean told me: "I fell in love with the Steinhatchee River and this rustic fishing village town and decided to build a vacation home here. Before long, Loretta and I were spending the majority of our spare time here. It occurred to me that it was mostly Georgia men that would come here to fish. They rarely brought their families because there wasn't much for families to do. I started thinking about what families would enjoy doing here. Then I started a scratch-pad list that evolved into the idea of a resort complex with the right amenities to attract families."

Dean had built nursing homes and retirement developments in Georgia, so he knew what a project like this entailed. He continued: "Condominium cracker boxes just wouldn't look right in this rustic little town, so I called the University of Florida School of Architecture to see if they had an expert in vintage Florida architecture. They

Steinhatchee River

introduced me to Professor Ron Haase who wrote a book called *Classic Cracker: Florida's Wood-Frame Vernacular Architecture.* Ron came up with the design criteria. He designed the first nine houses and the restaurant. Other architects have designed houses that are built here, but they follow the guidelines laid out by Ron."

On-site amenities include a swimming pool and spa, a children's playground, a farm-animal petting zoo, jogging trails, and tennis courts. They have canoes for exploring the river and will make arrangements for guided fishing and tours. Former president Jimmy Carter, a friend of Dean and Loretta's, brought his entire family—children and grandchildren—here for their 1996 Christmas family gathering. Reportedly, Mrs. Carter out-fished Jimmy.

General Zachary Taylor had ordered the building of Fort Frank Brooke alongside the Steinhatchee River in 1838, during the height of the Second Seminole War. There is convincing historical evidence that it was built very near, or possibly right on, the location of Steinhatchee Landing. In a *Gulf Coast Historical Review* article, historian Niles Schuh points out that reports and letters from army personnel who operated in this area during the Second Seminole War record that "...the falls of Steinhatchee River are six miles above Fort Frank Brooke." If their mileage estimates were accurate, this description would place the fort at the same bend in the river where Steinhatchee Landing is now. From the bottom of the river at the bend, scuba divers frequently bring up artifacts like utensils and buttons from military jackets.

Nearby Steinhatchee Falls can be reached by continuing northeast up State Road 51 about six miles to a dirt road on the right. Follow the dirt road for about a mile to the Steinhatchee River. The falls is really just an elevation change that speeds up the current over some rocks and creates a set of rapids, a rare sight in Florida. The river narrows here. Hundreds of years ago, this was the only spot where Timucuan Indians, and later Seminoles, could traverse the river on foot.

DIRECTIONS: From Highway 19, take SR 358 southwest to Jena and SR 361 north across the Steinhatchee River.

DON'T MISS: Steinhatchee Landing Resort

HIGH SPRINGS

Population: 4,717

*T*HE SANTA FE RIVER runs right by the town of High Springs. Poe Springs, Blue Springs, and Ginnie Springs are just a few miles east, off County Road 340. O'Leno State Park is just north of town on Highway 441. Ichetucknee Springs State Park is only fifteen miles northeast on Highway 27. The town of High Springs can rightly claim to be at the center of north central Florida's best springs and rivers. For canoeists, kayakers, tubers, scuba divers, and cave divers, it's the ideal bivouac. It can also be an interesting place to visit for non-aquatic types. Downtown High Springs' selection of antique shops draws day and weekend visitors from around the state.

In 1884, the Savannah, Florida, and Western Railroad extended its tracks from Live Oak south to Gainesville. They passed through a little community known as Santaffey, named after the Santa Fe River. The rail line put up a depot and a post office. Five years later, the townspeople changed the name to High Springs. (Apparently, there was once a spring on top of a hill in the middle of town.) The phosphate boom of the 1890s increased traffic, and a new rail, connecting High Springs with Tampa, opened in 1893. Two dozen trains were passing through each day. In 1896, Henry Plant's Plant System Railroad Line—which later merged with the Atlantic Coast Line—built a roundhouse where railroad cars could be pulled off the tracks. The company also built a steam-engine repair and maintenance shop, a boilermaker shop, a carpentry shop, and an ice house for icing down produce in the freight cars. The town's population swelled to more than three thousand. High Springs had become a major railroad repair depot. Today that original depot has been restored and now contains various business offices, and for a while it was home to one of Florida's best railroad museums.

After World War II, railroad lines began converting from steam-driven engines to diesel, and High Springs' railroad business evaporated. Three decades later, the town was rediscovered as a recreational hub because of the surrounding springs and rivers. In the mid-1980s, a downtown revitalization began with the first restoration of the brick, two-story Old Opera House building (originally built in 1895) on Main Street. In 2005, Bob and Karen Bentz bought the Opera House and spent two years renovating it again. In 2007 they reopened the Great Outdoors Restaurant with a more upscale décor and an all-new menu. The upstairs is now a banquet and conference center.

High Springs has attracted antiques shoppers for decades. Burch Antiques, next door to the old-fashioned Sheffield's Hardware, is a favorite. Check out the antique English stained-glass windows. Wisteria Cottage, Heartstrings, and High Springs Antiques Center are three others worth a visit.

Two fine bed and breakfasts can be found here as well. The Grady House, built in 1917, had previously been a bakery, a boarding house, and a private residence when Tony Boothby and Kirk Eppenstein bought and renovated it in 1998. A few years later they added the 1896 Easterlin Home next door. Paul and Lucie Regensdorf purchased it in 2006. Just outside of town you will find the Rustic Inn, where the grounds retain the feel of a gentleman's horse farm, which this property once was. A white pasture fence lines the front of the property. There's a horse pasture adjacent to the inn and a forest of planted pine trees, with a hiking path behind it. In its former life, the inn was a horse stable, although it has been so extensively renovated that you would never recognize it as such. It has six animal- and nature-themed rooms: the Cat Room, the Zebra Room, the Panda Room, the Everglades Room, the Tropical Room, and the Sea Mammals Room.

High Springs is a great place to visit, whether you're a river rat or an antiques hound.

DIRECTIONS: Take I-75 to the High Springs/Highway 441 exit. Go west on Highway 441.

DON'T MISS: Great Outdoors Trading Company and Restaurant

MICANOPY, CROSS CREEK, EVINSTON, MCINTOSH

Population: Micanopy 702; Cross Creek 50; Evinston 50; McIntosh 519

*I*F YOU HAVE SEEN the 1991 Michael J. Fox and Julie Warner movie *Doc Hollywood,* then you'll recognize Micanopy's main street, Cholokka Boulevard. Micanopy was the perfect double for the fictitious small southern town of Grady in the movie.

Micanopy dodged the modernization bullet back in the early 1960s when the Department of Transportation rerouted Highway 441 to run a couple miles east of town, rather than through it. When Interstate 75 was built a few years later, it too missed Micanopy by several miles to the west. As a result, four-block-long Cholokka Boulevard and the few residential blocks around it (as a whole declared a National Register Historic District in 1983) seem frozen in time. Huge oaks shade the town, and the brick storefronts on

Cholokka Boulevard look virtually the same as in photographs taken a hundred years ago. According to the Micanopy Historical Society Museum (a must-visit for history buffs), the town was established in 1821. It was called Wanton's Trading Post back then. However, the Seminole Indian village of Cuscowilla existed here long before that. Naturalist William Bartram reported visiting Cuscowilla in 1774. The town name changed to Micanopy in 1834, in honor of Seminole Chief Micanopy. It is likely the oldest inland town in Florida.

"Downtown" Micanopy is a wondrous find for curio shoppers, antiquers, and antiquarian book collectors, with more than a dozen unique shops. O. Brisky Books, in the brick 1885 Benjamin Building, has a vast inventory of old (and many rare) books, as well as a great selection of used and new Florida history and travel books. A block away, in the 1913 Mountain Garage Building, one atypical antique shop has an inventory of old tools and farm implements, and a fascinating collection of century-old medical devices. A couple shops specialize in old glassware—wine bottles, mason jars, and milk bottles. Across the street are the only two in-town eateries: the Old Florida Café, with well-stuffed sandwiches, salads, and a tasty "King Ranch" chili; and the Coffee N Cream Ice Cream Parlor for ice cream, coffee,

Cholokka Boulevard

baked goods, and sandwiches.

Overnight visitors will find Micanopy's Herlong Mansion everything a bed and breakfast should be: historic, elegant, quiet, inviting, and possibly haunted. This grand red-brick, Greek Revival-style southern plantation house features four massive Corinthian columns out front. The carefully renovated interior has the original leaded-glass windows; twelve-foot-high ceilings; mahogany, maple, and oak floors; quarter-sawn tiger-oak paneling; and ten fireplaces.

Herlong Mansion Bed & Breakfast

Zetty and Natalie Herlong moved to Natalie's family home in Micanopy in 1907 after their Alabama lumber business was destroyed in a fire. Natalie's parents, the Simontons, had built what was originally a two-story, wood-frame farm house back in the 1840s. But the Herlongs wanted something a bit grander, so in 1909 they remodeled by actually constructing this brick mansion on top of and around the original farm house.

The Herlongs re-started their lumber business in Micanopy and became prominent citrus farmers as well. When Natalie passed away in 1950, her six children inherited equal shares of the house, and an eighteen-year-long battle for sole ownership ensued. Eventually, sister Inez was granted legal possession. On the very first day of her ownership, while cleaning in the second-floor bedroom that she and her sister Mae had shared during childhood, Inez collapsed, went into a diabetic coma, and died shortly thereafter.

Occasionally over the years, guests and staff have reported the sound of footsteps or doors opening and closing upstairs when no one is there, usually in or around Mae's room.

Stephen and Carolyn West were ready for a change of pace after owning and operating the Eaton Lodge in Key West for eleven years when they found the Herlong Mansion for sale in 2006. "When we first came to see it, Stephen sat out on that lawn and stared at this place, and I could tell that he instantly loved it," Carolyn explains. "So I said OK, we'll do it." A big part of their decision to buy the Herlong Mansion was that much of the existing staff—who had worked here for many years and done an outstanding job—wanted to stay. While they haven't made any major changes, Stephen and Carolyn have added their touch to the décor, with some of their own tropical artwork and light airy drapes. "We wanted to make it a little brighter, more open-air, and comfortable." They redid much of the front landscaping as well, and received a landscaping award from the Alachua County Tourist Development Board for their efforts.

In keeping with the Southern ambiance, breakfast at the Herlong Mansion is a hearty affair. The menu varies daily, but expect big Southern breakfast items like buttermilk biscuits, cheese grits, scrambled eggs, sausage, ham, and breakfast casseroles. Micanopy is just twelve miles south of Gainesville, so for home-game football

Entrance to Marjorie Kinnan Rawlings' home

weekends the Herlong can be booked up a year in advance. Also adjacent to the house is the Herlong Mansion's separate banquet hall for weddings and conferences.

Visitors to Micanopy should not miss a side trip to Marjorie Kinnan Rawlings' home at Cross Creek, about a fifteen-minute drive east. One of Florida's most famous authors, Pulitzer Prize–winner Marjorie Rawlings wrote *The Yearling* and *Cross Creek,* among many other books and short stories, which depict both the humor and hardship of life in rural north-central Florida in the 1930s and 1940s. Rawlings' home (thought to have been built around 1890) and the surrounding property are now the Marjorie Kinnan Rawlings State Historic Site.

The Yearling and *The Secret River* were favorites of mine in elementary school. Years later I read *Cross Creek* and, from the first page, became so engrossed in Rawlings' world that I read it straight through, non-stop. She is funny, courageous, insightful, and almost supernatural in her understanding of both human nature and Mother Nature. She came to Cross Creek in 1928 to write gothic romance novels in seclusion. Instead, she found poignant drama in her own backyard. If you read *Cross Creek,* you will be compelled to go see the place that inspired it.

Cross Creek was fresh in my mind the first time I visited the Marjorie Kinnan Rawlings State Historic Site, and I marveled at how closely her real-life home matched the one in my imagination. Even the floor plan had a haunting sense of familiarity to me. I felt as if I had visited

Marjorie Kinnan Rawlings' home

this place in a dream and knew what to expect from room to room. Here is the front porch, where Marjorie sat countless hours before her typewriter and mixed the personalities she had come to know with the stories that she wove. *Jacob's Ladder, When the Whippoorwill—, Golden Apples, Cross Creek, The Sojourner,* and *The Yearling* all came to life in this very space. There is the birdbath in front of the house where, in the summer, redbirds would scold her for not replenishing it with fresh, cool water. Here is the screen door that her pet raccoon, Racket, learned to open and close for himself. Here is the indoor bathroom, added five years after she moved in, between the previously separate south side and north side of the house, whose sloping floor "has proved no friend to the aged, the absent-minded and the inebriated," as Marjorie once wrote.

Marjorie Rawlings died quite suddenly of a brain hemorrhage in 1953. She was only fifty-seven years old. Norton Baskin, Marjorie's second husband, had said that she had wanted to be buried at a small cemetery in Citra, just south of Island Grove. Apparently through some miscommunication between Norton and the funeral home, she was inadvertently buried in the wrong cemetery—Antioch Cemetery, down a dirt road east of Island Grove. Rawlings' grave is a simple, flat, marble slab with no headstone. No signs lead you to it. No fence surrounds it. Nothing distinguishes it from anyone else's grave. Her epitaph reads, "Marjorie Kinnan Rawlings, 1896–1953, Wife of Norton Baskin. Through her writing she endeared herself to the people of the world." On a more recent visit there, I found a new marble slab next to Marjorie's: "Norton Baskin, 1901–1997, Beloved Husband."

It was Marjorie Rawlings' wish that, after her passing, her house be kept as it was when she lived there, and the curators have done a marvelous job of honoring that request. She left it to the University of Florida Foundation, which maintained it from her death in 1953 until donating it to the Florida Department of Natural Resources in 1970.

Although there is no actual town at Cross Creek, there is a popular restaurant. The Yearling Restaurant opened in 1952. It was one of the first genuine Florida Cracker cuisine restaurants, serving such local fare as frog legs, gator tail, catfish, fried quail, collard greens, and cheese grits. The Yearling closed in 1992, but reopened in 2002 with its original ambiance and, most importantly, its authentic cuisine intact. The Yearling's fried gator tail is still the tastiest I've ever had.

1882 Wood & Swink Store and Post Office

Across Orange Lake from Cross Creek is the tiny community of Evinston (the "E" is pronounced as a short "I,"–"Ivinston"), home to the historic Wood & Swink Store and Post Office. Micanopy merchant S. H. Benjamin built the store in 1882 as a warehouse to store freight offloaded from the railroad. Two years later, the local postmaster purchased it and used it intermittently as a store and post office. In 1913, it became the permanent post office and today appears on the National Register of Historic Places. Fred Wood's book, *Evinston Home: God's Country,* was my source for some interesting local history.

In 1905, H. D. Wood and his brother-in-law, R. C. Evins, acquired the store following the hasty exit of the previous owner, John Hester. Apparently, while standing in the front door of his store, Hester shot and killed Watt Barron and wounded his father, J. F. Barron. One version of the story claims that the shooting resulted from an argument over who had the best-looking field of watermelons. Regardless of the cause, Hester was out and the Wood family was in. (In-law Paul Swink was a partner for just a couple years in the 1930s, but his name was left on the sign.) Descendent Fred Wood and his wife Wilma still run the store today. It is a time capsule, and thought to be Florida's oldest operating post office. Just inside the door stands a partition wall with a post office service window in the middle, surrounded by old-style post office boxes. Sixteen of them date back to 1882. An ancient cash register, a dozen jars of various home-pickled vegetables, and a row of fishbowl-shaped cookie jars sit atop a glass candy counter past the post office boxes. Tea, spices, cigars, and other general-store sundries sit on the shelves behind the counter. On the top shelf, several wooden boxes with "Winchester Small Arms Ammunition" stamped on the side look as though they have collected a few decades of dust. A big, old, wood-burning stove sits in the center of the store, surrounded by rocking chairs. If only that stove could speak.

The first time I came to Evinston, Wilma Wood introduced me to Jake and Pat Glisson, who live a few blocks from the store. The Glissons graciously invited me into their home (Pat had just made a batch of Christmas cookies) to interview Jake. Jake Glisson is an accomplished artist and book author who grew up next door to Marjorie Rawlings. She wrote about the Glisson family in *Cross Creek.*

A young Jake and Marjorie became close friends, even though his dad and Marjorie did not always see eye to eye.

In Jake Glisson's 1993 book, *The Creek,* he tells marvelous stories that illustrate what life was like for a kid growing up in Cross Creek. He was a firsthand witness to many of the events about which Marjorie wrote, so some of his stories overlap with hers, but he tells them from his own viewpoint—sometimes to the consternation of Marjorie Rawlings scholars. He explained to me, "I thought that writers in a historical society would be interested in the license that Mrs. Rawlings used in writing, for instance, *Cross Creek.* Just that slight little deviation that can change the meaning, and in some cases was a little imaginary. I feel that it was part of her brilliance, that she did a little patchwork here and there, ever so delicately." Jake's love and respect for Marjorie Rawlings are apparent, particularly in his chapter "That Woman Next Door." Jake's point was that sometimes writers adjust things a little to make them fit, and Marjorie was no different in that respect. The opportunity to reread those stories from a different viewpoint is one of the things that make his book so fascinating. Jake told me that writing *The Creek* was a return to his childhood. "The truth is, the day I finished the book I was a little depressed," he said. "Because in writing it, it was kind of like I went back there and did it all again. It was a fun experience."

Between Micanopy and Ocala, Highway 441 rolls across scenic pasture land and into the tranquil and historic hamlet of McIntosh, on the west side of Orange Lake. Avenue G, with the town's only traffic light, is a good place to start your visit.

Huge live oaks grace every yard, their Spanish moss–covered limbs spreading out over the tops of homes and across streets. They must be centuries old. Some have trunks as big around as small houses (and look as though Keebler elves live inside them). I've never seen so many grand oak trees in one place. Two of the grandest are on Avenue G in the front yard and backyard of what was once Margie Karow's Merrily Bed and Breakfast. W. E. Allen, McIntosh's first postmaster, built the house in 1888. Sadly, on a recent visit I learned that Margie Karow had passed away in April 2010 at 87 years old.

Most of the other houses along McIntosh's avenues (B through H) are also one-hundred-plus-year-old Victorians—some restored, some

1884 McIntosh Railroad Depot Historical Museum

not. They were originally the homes of citrus and cotton farmers whose fields surrounded the town. After the big freezes of 1894 and 1895, the farmers switched to vegetables–crookneck squash, cabbage, lettuce. I'm told that the old Gist House, at the corner of Avenue H and Fifth Street, was built with the revenues of a single season's crookneck squash crop. Another farmer grew iceberg lettuce exclusively for the ocean liner Queen Mary and shipped it by train to New York.

At the end of Avenue G is McIntosh's restored railroad depot. Originally constructed in 1884 by the old Florida Southern Railroad, it was scheduled to be torn down in 1974. In 1973, a group of townsfolk who felt the depot was a valuable landmark formed the Friends of McIntosh to try to save it. It is now McIntosh's Historical Museum.

McIntosh postmaster Sharon Little is one of the original founders of the Friends of McIntosh. She moved here in 1972 and became postmaster in 1981. Sharon told me: "We formed the Friends of McIntosh in nineteen-seventy-three just to save the depot. We needed to purchase it from the railroad and move it six feet back from the track. Six thousand dollars is what we had to come up with, and we decided that the best way to raise that would be to hold a little festival right here in the park. Our first Eighteen-Nineties Festival was in nineteen-seventy-four. We had twenty-five vendors and drew about thirty-five hundred people." The 1890s Festival has run every year since, on either the third or fourth weekend in October (so as not to conflict with a University of Florida Gators game). It now draws forty thousand people and features tours of McIntosh's historic homes, storytelling, a parade, more than three hundred vendors, and all-day live entertainment.

Visitors to McIntosh will find hearty sustenance at Agnes O-Steen's Antique Deli, at the corner of Highway 441 and G Street, and two miles south on 441 at Rocky's Villa, Italian and Mexican Diner.

DIRECTIONS: **Micanopy:** Take I-75 to Micanopy exit # 374, County Road 234. Go east to Seminary Street, and south into Micanopy.

Cross Creek: From Highway 441, take CR 346 east to CR 325 and turn south. The Marjorie Kinnan Rawlings State Historic Site is four miles down on the right.

Evinston: From Highway 441 (south of Micanopy), go east on County Road 10.

McIntosh: Go six miles south of Micanopy on Highway 441.

DON'T MISS: The Marjorie Kinnan Rawlings State Historic Site in Cross Creek

CRESCENT CITY, WELAKA

Population: Crescent City 1,782; Welaka 788

SCENIC US 17 ROLLS though fern-growing country north of DeLand and brings you to Crescent City, which rests atop a bluff on the curved (hence "Crescent") west bank of Crescent Lake.

The first families settled here in 1852, and a few more came in the late 1860s. In 1875, Charles Griffing bought most of the property and divided it into single-acre home lots and five-acre citrus groves. Griffing's wife, Jennie, changed the name of what was then Dunn's Lake to Crescent Lake because its shape reminded her of the crescent moon. The new town adopted the name of the lake.

US Route 17 becomes Summit Street when it passes through downtown Crescent City. Turn east onto Central Avenue and follow it four blocks downhill to Crescent Lake and you'll find docks with covered boathouses lining the shore. This lake, like many others, once claimed to be "the bass capital of the world." However, Crescent City's big annual event is the Catfish Festival, held the first weekend in April. The agenda includes bluegrass music, arts and crafts displays, and a parade, but the highlight is the catfish skinning contest.

There are some interesting turn-of-the-century homes near and along the waterfront. One is Sprague House, a couple of blocks up from the lake at 125 Central Avenue. Built in 1892 by a local citrus farmer, it was purchased in 1902 by the town's mayor, Dr. Guilford Sprague, and his wife, Kate, who ran it as an inn. Famous former guests include William Jennings Bryant and Theodore Roosevelt. Current innkeepers Jeff and Amy Hastin have once again turned this charming Victorian, with two-story wrap-around porches and stained glass windows, into an inn, The Sprague House Bed & Breakfast.

Continuing north on Highway 17, then heading west on Putnam County Road 308B will bring you to Welaka, the real "bass capital." Welaka, a variation of the Seminole Indian name for the St. Johns River, *Ylacco*, sits on a bluff overlooking the St. Johns at one of its most scenic points. Bass-fishing enthusiasts rent boats or bring their own and stay at rustic fishing lodges and cabins on the river, like Andersen's Lodge, and the less rustic Floridian Sports Club. There's good fresh seafood at these places too.

DIRECTIONS: Drive north from DeLand on US 17 to Crescent City. Continue north on US 17 to CR 308B, then turn west to CR 309 and Welaka.

DON'T MISS: The Sprague House Bed & Breakfast

CEDAR KEY

Population: 954

*F*LORIDA'S FIRST CROSS-STATE railroad ended way out here. German pencil company founder Eberhard Faber found red cedar pencil wood way out here. John Muir finished his thousand-mile walk from Indiana to the Gulf of Mexico way out here. Jimmy Buffet played in the Neptune Bar at the Island Hotel way out here (way back when he only got airtime on country stations). Way out here the Gulf of Mexico is shallow, mud-and-oyster-shell-bottomed, and sprinkled with half a dozen small islands. The town is called Cedar Key, but it's actually on Way Key—once a "way" station for sailing vessels to re-supply and drop ballast. It's fair to describe Cedar Key as way out there—geographically, artistically, and attitudinally.

As with many of Florida's towns, a railroad is what brought

2nd Street

commerce to Cedar Key. Florida's first cross-state railroad, the Atlantic to Gulf/Florida Railroad Company Line, completed in 1861, ran from Fernandina to Cedar Key. Cedar milling was the dominant industry here from the 1870s through the 1890s. Pencil manufacturer A. W. Faber had a mill on Atsena Otie Key, half a mile offshore from Way Key. Naturally, seafood has always figured prominently in Cedar Key's economy. Today this area is the largest producer of farm-raised clams in the country.

The drive down Highway 24 from Otter Creek to Cedar Key is long and straight. If you're traveling it on the third weekend in October or the third weekend in April, you will likely run into a traffic jam miles before you reach town. Cedar Key's October Seafood Festival and April Old Florida Arts Festival are two of the oldest and most popular such events in the state. They're terrific festivals, but don't expect to see much of the town or to soak up its offbeat character while they're going on. Any other time you'll probably have the highway to yourself, and the most traffic you will encounter in town will be a bicycle or an occasional old pickup truck on 2nd Street. Cedar Key moves at an unhurried pace—dictated mostly by whim or the weather, hence its quirky charm.

Cedar Key's most famous landmark, the Island Hotel, stands near the east end of 2nd Street, Cedar Key's four-block-long main street. The building was originally Parsons and Hale's General Store when it was built in 1859. It survived hostile Union troop occupation during the Civil War, and its oak-beam frame and one-foot-thick tabby walls have stood up to floods; numerous hurricanes, including the devastating 1896 Hurricane; and fires, including one started by the hotel's owner during the Great Depression (the fire department was just across the street, and firemen saved it). Before he moved to California and founded the Sierra Club, naturalist John Muir hiked from Indiana down to Cedar Key, where he stayed for several months in 1867 while recuperating from malaria. Muir described Parsons and Hale's General Store in his journal, writing: "I stepped into a little store, which had a considerable trade in quinine, and alligator and rattlesnake skins. . . ."

In 1915, Simon Feinberg, a property investor, bought the building and remodeled it into the Bay Hotel. In the years that followed, the hotel changed names and owners frequently.

Today the rustic ten-room Island Hotel looks very much the same as it did in photographs from the 1940s. Everyone seems to agree that the hotel's heyday began in 1946, when Bessie and Loyal Gibbs bought the inn (by then it had degraded into a honky-tonk brothel). They remodeled the place and named it the Island Hotel. Loyal—aka "Gibby"—ran the bar, and Bessie, a superb chef, ran the restaurant. She is credited with invention of the Hearts of Palm Salad. Today the Island Hotel Restaurant is one of the best restaurants in town, and it still serves Bessie's original recipe Hearts of Palm Salad. Another specialty is its soups—Crab Bisque is always on the menu, and if Chilled Melon is the soup du jour, don't miss it.

Another popular restaurant, Tony's Seafood, in the circa 1880s Hale Building at the west end of 2nd Street, serves some sumptuous dishes like Grilled Teriyaki Mahi-mahi, Steamed Blue Crabs, and the local requisite, Steamed Clams.

Stroll along 2nd Street and you'll find more hundred-and-fifty-year-old buildings, with arts-and-craft shops and galleries, as well as the Cedar Key Historical Society's museum.

Tony's Seafood Restaurant, Historic Hale Building

Artists have been finding Cedar Key's eclectic ambiance creatively conducive for decades, and many have made it their home. At Cedar Keyhole Artist Co-op and Gallery on 2nd Street, local artists display and sell a wide range of art, from pottery (like Ron Dahline's expressive face jugs), to paintings (like Russell Raethka's fish and local scenery watercolors).

Two blocks south of 2nd, on Dock Street, you'll find tourist gift shops, more galleries, and several casual bar-and-grill eateries in a collection of ramshackle sea-weathered wood buildings that hang out over the water. The eateries all have similar menus—fried fish, shrimp, and clams.

For lodging, in addition to the Island Hotel, there is the Cedar Key Bed & Breakfast, which occupies the tin-roofed, two-story historic Wadley House. The Eagle Cedar Mill built it as an employee residence in 1880, at the height of Cedar Key's cedar industry

Stilt shack off Cedar Key

boom. For a while, the daughter of David Yulee (Florida's first U.S. Senator and builder of the Atlantic to Gulf/Florida Railroad) operated a boarding house out of it. Today's owners, Bill and Alice Phillips, purchased it in 2003. Two Dock Street lodging alternatives are the Harbour Master Suites (eight rooms with private balconies overlooking the Gulf) and the Sawgrass Motel (just two rooms overlooking the activity on Dock Street).

Not many towns this small can boast two historical museums. The Cedar Key Historical Society operates a museum in the 1871 Lutterloh Building at the corner of State Road 24 and 2nd Street. And the Cedar Key State Museum is off Way Key, and a little more difficult to find. Just follow the signs, which are everywhere in town.

DIRECTIONS: From Highway 19, turn southwest on Highway 24 at Otter Creek.

DON'T MISS: The Island Hotel

ROSEWOOD, FLORIDA

Racial violence erupted in the small and quiet Rosewood
community January 1-7, 1923. Rosewood, a predominantly colored
community, was home to the Bradley, Carrier, Carter, Goins, and
Hall families, among others. Residents supported a school taught
by Mahulda "Gussie" Brown Carrier, three churches, and a Masonic
lodge. Many of them owned their homes, some were business
owners, and others worked in nearby Sumner and at the Cummer
Lumber Mill. This quiet life came to an end on January 1, 1923,
when a white Sumner woman accused a black man of assaulting
her. In the search for her alleged attacker, whites terrorized and
killed Rosewood residents. In the days of fear and violence that
followed, many Rosewood citizens sought refuge in the nearby
woods. White merchant John M. Wright and other courageous
whites sheltered some of the fleeing men, women and children.
Whites burned Rosewood and looted livestock and property; two
were killed while attacking a home. Five blacks also lost their lives:
Sam Carter, who was tortured for information and shot to death
on January 1; Sarah Carrier, Lexie Gordon, James Carrier, and
Mingo Williams. Those who survived were forever scarred.
(Continued on other side)

A FLORIDA HERITAGE LANDMARK
SPONSORED BY THE REAL ROSEWOOD FOUNDATION, INC.
AND THE FLORIDA DEPARTMENT OF STATE

ROSEWOOD

Population: 0

*A*BOUT TEN MINUTES EAST of Cedar Key on Highway
24, you will come across a historical marker for Rosewood. Other
than a few scattered bricks and boards in the woods close by, there
are no structural remains of the original Rosewood community. But
the marker, dedicated by Governor Jeb Bush in 1994, gives a brief
description of the horrific tragedy that took place nearby in January
1923. The village of Rosewood, established in 1845, was originally
populated by both blacks and whites who worked mostly in red cedar harvesting and milling. By the 1890s most of the red cedar was
gone. The pencil mills in Cedar Key were closed, and Rosewood's
population shrank. Most (but not all) of the families that remained
were black. They found work in the local turpentine industry. Some

started their own businesses. They built a school, three churches, a train station, a general store, and a Masonic lodge. They even had a community baseball team—the Rosewood Stars. It was a small, quiet, hard-working community. On New Year's Day, 1923, a white woman living in nearby Sumner claimed she had been assaulted by a black man—a dubious claim, according to historians. A search for the alleged assailant was joined by Klu Klux Klan members who had been at a march in Gainesville the day before, and it quickly escalated into a vigilante invasion of Rosewood. It was a bloody massacre. The village was destroyed, and eight people—six black and two white—were killed.

DIRECTIONS: Drive eight miles east of Cedar Key on Highway 24.

CENTRAL REGION

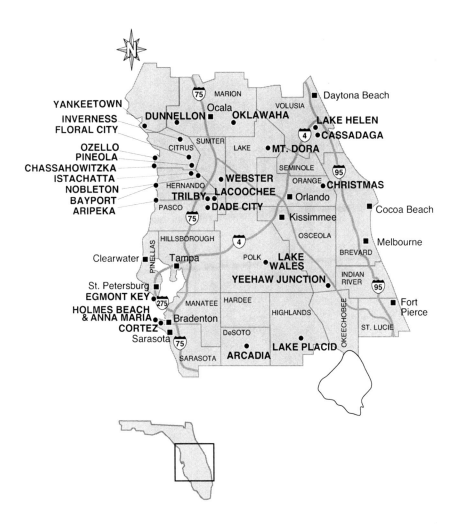

YANKEETOWN
INVERNESS
FLORAL CITY
OZELLO
PINEOLA
CHASSAHOWITZKA
ISTACHATTA
NOBLETON
BAYPORT
ARIPEKA

75 MARION
Ocala
DUNNELLON OKLAWAHA
VOLUSIA
Daytona Beach
LAKE HELEN
4 CASSADAGA
SUMTER
CITRUS
LAKE
MT. DORA
SEMINOLE
95
HERNANDO
WEBSTER
ORANGE
CHRISTMAS
LACOOCHEE
TRILBY
DADE CITY
Orlando
PASCO
75
Kissimmee
Cocoa Beach
OSCEOLA
Melbourne
4
BREVARD
Clearwater
PINELLAS
Tampa
POLK
LAKE
WALES
YEEHAW JUNCTION
INDIAN
RIVER
95
St. Petersburg
EGMONT KEY
275
MANATEE
HARDEE
Fort
Pierce
HOLMES BEACH
& ANNA MARIA
Bradenton
HIGHLANDS
ST. LUCIE
CORTEZ
Sarasota
75
DeSOTO
OKEECHOBEE
ARCADIA
LAKE PLACID
SARASOTA

YANKEETOWN

Population: 680

FLORIDA'S BIG BEND AREA—now officially called the Nature Coast and sometimes unofficially referred to as the Cracker Coast—starts somewhere north of New Port Richey and curves around to somewhere east of Lighthouse Point, south of Tallahassee. What distinguishes it from the rest of Florida's coast is that there are, with just a couple small exceptions, no beaches here. The sea bottom, extending for miles out into the Gulf of Mexico, is seldom deeper than ten feet; because of this shallow shelf, there is very little wave action to build up a beach. Without beaches, there are no high-rise condos or hotels, fewer T-shirt shops, and fewer Bermuda shorts–clad tourists. The Big Bend coastline is mostly grass flats and marsh. Some of Florida's most scenic spring-fed rivers empty into the Gulf in this stretch, and some lightly populated fishing villages have grown up around these areas. Yankeetown is one of these. It meanders, like a snake, alongside the Withlacoochee for about six miles, a few miles inland from the Gulf.

Yankeetown experienced brief national fame twice during the 1960s. First, during the 1960 Nixon-Kennedy presidential campaigns, the townsfolk held a debate and a straw election. The news wires picked up the story, and it was a national topic for several days. Nixon won in Yankeetown.

Yankeetown's second brush with fame came in the summer of 1961, when the Mirisch Company and United Artists came here to make a movie based on Richard Powell's novel *Pioneer, Go Home*. For the big screen, the title was changed to *Follow That Dream*. It starred Elvis Presley, who stayed in Yankeetown for two months. Elvis fans came from far and wide to see their idol making his ninth major motion picture. Extra traffic police had to be brought in to keep the crowds at bay. One of the main film set locations was a bridge where County Road 40 crosses Bird Creek about a mile from where it dead-ends into the Gulf. Locals have renamed County Road 40 from Highway 19 west the Follow That Dream Parkway.

See Yankeetown! signs, each made from a single horizontal board with one end sawed to a point, could be found alongside many of north Florida's and south Georgia's rutted roads in the 1920s and 1930s, long before *See Rock City!* became a common sight. They advertised a riverside retreat at Honey Bluff along the Withlacoochee River. The original name for the retreat was going to be Knotts, named after A. F. Knotts, a U. S. Steel Corporation attorney, former Indiana state representative, and former mayor of Hammond, Indiana. After his retirement, Knotts came to Florida in search of a place to build a camp for fishing and hunting, preferably on a navigable freshwater stream.

Knotts had handled all the land transactions when U. S. Steel built the town of Gary, Indiana, in 1905, so he was quite familiar with founding communities. Initially, he purchased some property on Crystal River, but in 1920 found that he liked the Honey Bluff area on the Withlacoochee River better. He advertised the location to his friends back in Indiana, and some came and built shanties alongside

Izaak Walton Lodge

the river. To get there they had to travel by rail to Dunnellon, then ride twenty-five miles to the coast with Hugh Coleman, the Star Route mail carrier. It was Coleman who started calling the place Yankeetown, since he was carrying so many Yankees to Knotts' fishing camp. The name stuck. A. F.'s nephew, Eugene Knotts, suggested they build a lodge on the river to be run by Eugene and his wife, Norma, to accommodate shorter-term visitors. Completed in 1924, this would become the Izaak Walton Lodge, appropriately named after seventeenth-century English author Sir Izaak Walton, best known for *The Compleat Angler,* his treatise on the art and virtues of fishing and in praise of a simpler and more leisurely lifestyle.

Wayne and Linda Harrington purchased and renovated the Izaak Walton Lodge in 1987, and opened the exceptional Compleat Angler Restaurant there, overlooking a bend in the Withlacoochee River. But on July 22, 1999, disaster struck when the wooden lodge caught fire. Except for the kitchen, most of the building was destroyed. The Harringtons, ever determined, rebuilt and reopened both the lodge and the restaurant fourteen months later. The new lodge, while not an exact replica, pays fine homage to the original.

In recent years, strong controversy has come to Yankeetown. In 2006, a group of developers—most from Clearwater—purchased the lodge and the marina property next door with the intention of building a condominium and marina complex. There is strong opposition from the residents of Yankeetown. As of this writing, the battle is ongoing. I list two Yankeetown websites in the Appendix: one is the developers' site for the property, and the other is the residents' "Save Yankeetown" site.

DIRECTIONS: From Highway 19, turn west at Inglis on CR 40.

DON'T MISS: The Izaak Walton Lodge (hopefully it will still be there)

DUNNELLON

Population: 1,933

*T*HE QUIET AGRICULTURAL TOWN of Dunnellon, at the confluence of the Withlacoochee and Rainbow rivers, found itself transformed into a mining boomtown overnight in 1889. That year, while digging a well in his backyard, Albertus Vogt discovered a vein of extraordinarily pure hard-rock phosphate. He took a sample to Ocala railroad man John F. Dunn, who promptly bought a half interest in the property owned by Albertus and his brother John. The Dunnellon Phosphate Company (named for Dunn's wife, Ellen) was born. One year later, the town of Dunnellon incorporated, and then almost overnight it experienced the same transformation that Wild West towns had gone through during the Gold Rush. Schemers and scam artists smelled quick money and moved in. Saloons and brothels went up by the dozens. Saturday night street gunfights were commonplace. It was a slice of the Wild West in the Deep South, but it would not last forever.

The boom era, and the lawlessness that accompanied it, faded after the turn of the century. Then it disappeared completely when the European market for phosphate stopped with the onset of World War I. Dunnellon returned to its quiet-community status. Around 1930, F. E. Hemphill and Frank Greene began to develop an area about three miles north of town that included the Rainbow Springs basin (known then as Blue Springs). They built a lodge, a pavilion, and a dock for a glass-bottom boat. The springs changed hands a number of times over the next several decades. In the late 1960s, Holiday Inn and S & H Greenstamps jointly purchased the property and further developed it as a tourist theme park, complete with a monorail ride, glass-bottom boats, a paddle-wheel riverboat called the *Rainbow Queen,* and wild animal exhibits. But when Interstate 75 was built, it bypassed Dunnellon to the east by twenty-two miles. Tourist traffic dried up, and the Rainbow Springs attraction closed its doors in 1974.

The community of Dunnellon knew that it had something special in Rainbow Springs, however. It is a first-magnitude spring with the fourth highest volume in Florida and a year-round water temperature of 73 degrees. The Rainbow River's clear waters are filled with bass and bream. The spring is a wonderful natural resource that Dunnellon's residents could not stand to see go to waste. They wanted it to be accessible to the community, but they also wanted it to be preserved (and not as a theme park). Through the latter 1980s, a group of volunteers from Dunnellon and Citrus Springs and the Village of Rainbow Springs Garden Club worked diligently to restore the park, all at their own expense. Ultimately, they were able to convince the State of Florida to purchase the property in 1990 and turn it into a state park. In 1992, Rainbow Springs State Park opened on weekends only, with major financial and volunteer help from the community. In March 1995, it celebrated its grand opening as a full-time state park—one of the state's most scenic. The monorail, riverboat, and glass-bottom boats are long gone, but what's left is the natural beauty that has always been here.

K. P. Hole County Park, just south of Rainbow Springs State Park, is the best place to rent tubes, kayaks, and canoes. If you want to pack a picnic lunch, I found a terrific little café in town with great sandwiches, soups, and salads—Abigail's Café & Coffee Shop, on Pennsylvania Avenue.

DIRECTIONS: From I-75 go west on Highway 484 to Dunnellon. From Dunnellon, go four miles north on Highway 41 to Rainbow Springs State Park.

DON'T MISS: Rainbow Springs State Park

OCKLAWAHA

Population: 1,000

*O*NE HOUR BEFORE DAWN on the morning of January 16, 1935, residents of the sleepy central Florida town of Ocklawaha simultaneously bolted upright in their beds, startled from their deep slumber by the rapid and continuous blasting of machine guns. It continued without pause for forty-five minutes and then went on sporadically for another five hours, until FBI agents decided that notorious gangsters Ma Barker and her son Fred were surely dead.

Ocklawaha is a place far enough off the beaten path that if you were so inclined, you could hide away here for some time without being found. Arizona Clark "Ma" Barker, also known as Kate, must have had that same impression when she came here in November 1934 and rented a two-story, wood-frame house on the shore of Lake

Weir under the alias Mrs. T. C. Blackburn.

Ocklawaha probably looked much the same then as it does now. It's a one-caution-light town on the north shore of Lake Weir, about twenty miles southeast of Ocala. There's a new Lake Weir Chamber of Commerce office, the Lake Weir Community Building next door, a small city park, and the Lake Weir grocery, all on CR 25, the main road through town. Turn down SE 135th Avenue to the shore of Lake Weir and you'll find Gator Joe's Beach Bar and Grill in an old 1926 stilt building. They specialize in Florida Cracker cuisine—gator tail, frog's legs, and oysters—as well as shrimp, grouper sandwiches, and burgers. Lake Weir is a popular summer water-skiing and fishing spot. Lake cabins and docks line the shore, and Gator Joe's is at the center of the activity.

Back out on CR 25, heading west, look carefully for a small wooden sign that says "Harper's Place" at a dirt drive on the left. It is private property, so stop here to get a distant glimpse of the Barker Gang house. It's a simple white, wood-frame two-story with a screened porch downstairs—no different from a dozen other older houses along the shore at this end of Lake Weir. No different, except that seventy-odd years ago, the reign of one of history's most infamous gangs ended in a bloody gun battle here.

The Barker boys—Herman, Lloyd, Arthur (who was called "Doc"), and Fred—had always been bad eggs. As kids, they were bullies and thieves in their hometown of Webb City, Missouri, and later in Tulsa, Oklahoma. They spent most of their formative years in scrapes with the law. Ma, who as a child had seen in person and idolized Jesse James, not only tolerated these activities but encouraged them. She ultimately organized the Barkers into a criminal gang.

In 1922, police officers caught Lloyd during a post office holdup and sent him to Leavenworth. In 1927, the oldest brother, Herman, shot himself rather than be captured following a gun battle with police in Wichita, Kansas. Undaunted, the Barker Gang continued its crime spree. The gang was joined by Alvin "Old Creepy" Karpis (nicknamed because of his menacing expression), a former Kansas State Penitentiary inmate and associate of Fred's. For a while, bank robberies were their specialty, and they always left a trail of dead bodies behind—policemen, innocent bystanders, and sometimes fellow criminals. Then the Barkers figured out that there was more money in kidnapping than bank robbery when they abducted William Hamm Jr. of the Hamm Brewing Company in St. Paul, Minnesota. They collected $100,000 ransom for his release in June 1933. In January 1934, Fred and Old Creepy kidnapped wealthy St. Paul banker Edward Bremer. Bremer's family paid $200,000, and he was returned unharmed.

By now the Barker Gang was at the top of the FBI's Most Wanted list. They were on the run. They even went so far as to have a doctor accomplice try to surgically alter their faces and scrape their fingers so their prints would be unrecognizable. The gang split and went in different directions to try to foil the FBI. That may have been the beginning of their downfall.

In January 1935 in Chicago, FBI agent Melvin Purvis caught Doc and sent him to Alcatraz. In Doc's apartment, agents found a map of Florida with a circle drawn around Ocala and Lake Weir. Ultimately, however, it was the Barkers' cruelty to animals that pinpointed their location for the FBI.

When Ma and Fred Barker (a.k.a. the Blackburns) first settled in Ocklawaha, they were considered friendly by the locals. They were regulars and big tippers at the bar. But before long, boredom got the best of Fred, and he took to shooting at ducks on Lake Weir with his machine gun. This did not set well with the locals. When Fred let it be known that he wanted to hunt down "Old Joe," a legendary but harmless old alligator that lived in the lake, the locals were enraged, and word of his intentions spread. His description matched one given by the FBI, and in the early morning of January 16, fourteen agents surrounded the house.

Chief Agent E. J. Connelly announced, "We're from the Department of Justice. Come out one at a time."

Ma barker yelled, "All right, Freddie! Go ahead!" and the Barkers opened fire. FBI agents fired over fifteen hundred rounds of bullets into the house in three-quarters of an hour and then continued to shoot through the windows intermittently for several more hours. When they finally went inside, they found Ma and Fred dead on the floor of the bullet-ridden upstairs bedroom. They also found an arsenal of rifles, machine guns, pistols, and ammunition. Ma still clutched her machine gun in her hands.

A year later, J. Edgar Hoover caught up with Alvin Karpis in New Orleans. Karpis spent thirty-two years in prison. Ten years after his release, he died of a drug overdose. Lloyd Barker served a twenty-five-year sentence and then was shot by his wife two years after his release. In 1939, Doc Barker attempted to escape from Alcatraz. He made it over the walls and was standing on the shore of the island when guards fatally shot him.

DIRECTIONS: From Highway 441, south of Ocala, turn east at Belleview on CR 25.

DON'T MISS: A peek at the Barker Gang house from the road

CASSADAGA, LAKE HELEN

Population: Cassadaga 200 (estimate); Lake Helen 2,771

*O*NE HUNDRED FORTY YEARS AGO, self-proclaimed spiritualist George Colby was financially destitute and in poor health. Colby claimed that, during a séance, an Indian spirit guide named Seneca had instructed him to take a journey south, despite his situation. Seneca advised him to build a community where other spiritualists could learn, live, and teach. First, he must go by way of Wisconsin. In Wisconsin, Colby met T. D. Giddings. In another séance, Seneca directed the two of them specifically to go to Florida. Colby and Giddings' family settled on a lake in wild central Florida that Colby claimed he had envisioned in the séance. In 1880, he built a home and filed for homestead on seventy-four and a half acres. Homestead was granted four years later, but Colby didn't stay. He set out across the country to lecture and hold séances. It was not until 1894 that a group from New York approached George Colby about organizing the Southern Cassadaga Spiritualist Camp Meeting Association. In January 1895, he deeded thirty-five acres of his property to the Association, and the community of Cassadaga was born. They held their first camp meeting the following month in Colby's home.

Cassadaga must have been at least somewhat financially successful for Colby and Giddings, although that was not its purpose. George Colby was able to live there for most of the balance of his life as the town's main spiritual advisor. Early writings about nearby Lake Helen describe T. D. Giddings' house as prominent and the first to have "real glass windows."

Originally, Cassadaga was just a winter retreat for psychics from up north. As more people arrived around the turn of the century, the Association began leasing plots of land to them to build their own homes on. This owned-house-on-leased-land arrangement still exists with most of the homeowners today. Most all of the town's residents are still today spiritualists, and many are mediums or psychics. Cassadaga's current fifty-seven acres have been designated a historic district on the National Register of Historic Places.

The Association defines a spiritualist as "one who believes, as the basis of his or her religion, in the communication of this and the spirit world by means of mediumship, and who endeavors to mold his or her character and conduct in accordance with the highest teachings derived from such communion." Mediums, of course, are those who communicate with the spirit world.

If reading your horoscope in the newspaper just isn't telling you enough, then maybe a trip to Cassadaga is in order. By appointment at the Cassadaga Hotel, anyone can book a session with one of the on-duty psychics. Depending on the psychic's best-developed abilities, he or she will divine your future by reading Tarot cards, your palm, or your aura. Psychics may also interpret your dreams, and in a longer session, some will do a past-life regression.

The current two-story Cassadaga Hotel was built in 1928 (the original burned in a fire in 1926) and is the town's centerpiece. Some of the rooms are reserved for sessions, but the rest are available for lodging. The Lost In Time Café in the hotel lobby serves a fine

Cassadaga Hotel

assortment of sandwiches, soups, and salads.

Across the street in the 1905 Andrew Jackson Davis Building, you will find the Cassadaga Camp Bookstore and Gift Shop, with a sizeable selection of new-age books and music CDs.

From the hotel it is worthwhile to take a walk down the narrow streets of Cassadaga and look at the houses. Most are brightly painted gingerbread cottages, though some are obscured by overgrown vines and overhanging Spanish moss and thus seem a bit creepy. Most have a "Medium" or "Spiritual Guidance" shingle hanging out front.

On a visit to Cassadaga in 2010, I was disappointed to discover that one of my favorite bed & breakfasts, the Ann C. Stevens House, had closed. The property was part of George Colby's original homestead. He sold it to Stevens, a fellow spiritualist and farm owner from Michigan. Stevens Street in Cassadaga is named for her. The circa 1895 house is listed on the National Register of Historic Places.

A couple miles down County Road 4139, you will come to the town of Lake Helen, whose historic district, particularly along Euclid Avenue, has a number of beautifully restored turn-of-the-century homes. One standout is a majestic three-story Victorian plantation home called Edgewood at 214 Euclid Avenue. Cincinnati architect and builder John Porter Mace brought his family to Lake Helen in 1885. He built Edgewood as their home, and he designed and built many of the other homes in Lake Helen as well. Mace was the town's first mayor and a major contributor to Lake Helen's development. He owned a lumberyard and a sawmill, and was also one of the largest orange growers and packers in the county. The brand name for his oranges was Edgewood.

Lake Helen has one of my favorite small-town libraries, which hosts one the state's best Florida authors book fairs each March. In 2008, restoration of the original (next door to the current) Lake Helen Hopkins Library building, built in 1897, was completed.

DIRECTIONS: From I-4, take the Orange City/Blue Springs/Cassadaga/Highway 472 exit (Exit 54). Go northeast 1/3 mile on Highway 472 to CR 4101. Go right for a couple hundred yards, then turn right again at CR 4139/Cassadaga Road and follow it back across the I-4 overpass into Cassadaga. Continue on CR 4139/Macy Avenue another mile into Lake Helen.

DON'T MISS: A stroll through the neighborhood streets of Cassadaga

MOUNT DORA

Population: 13,650

*M*OUNT DORA, FLORIDA, may not actually be in the mountains, but it does snow here–at least one day a year. On the second Saturday in December, the city's Parks & Recreation Department sponsors Children's Christmas in the Park in downtown Mount Dora's Donnelly Park, where the big attraction is a snow-making machine. It's all part of a month of non-stop Christmas festivities that take place each December in Mount Dora.

Quaint, picturesque, and although not mountainous, at least hilly, Mount Dora is only forty-five minutes north of Orlando, but a century away in time. It could easily be Florida's version of Bedford Falls (in the movie *It's a Wonderful Life*). Victorian homes, a postcard-perfect turn-of-the-century main street, antique shops, superb restaurants,

Donnelly Street

and inviting bed & breakfasts make Mount Dora one of Florida's most-visited small towns. It has become famous for festivals: arts and music festivals in February, an antique boat festival in March, and the annual bicycle festival in October. But the town's most festive time is Christmas.

Mount Dora can trace its history to the late 1800s, when a local postmaster, Ross Tremain, provisionally named the small community of homesteaders Royellou—a combination of the names of his three children. After a few years the name changed to Mount Dora. The "Dora" in Mount Dora was Dora Ann Drawdy, one of the area's first homesteaders back in the 1840s.

The town began to develop in earnest when James Alexander, John MacDonald, and J. P. Donnelly opened a ten-room inn overlooking Lake Dora in 1883. They named it the Alexander House, but subsequent owners would rename it the Lake House, then the Lakeside Inn, which it remains today. One historical highlight is that in the winter of 1930, Calvin Coolidge came to the inn for an extended sabbatical with his wife following his just-completed term as president. During his stay, he dedicated the newly completed Gables and Terrace wings. James Barggren and Richard Dempsey bought

Lakeside Inn

the Lakeside Inn in 1992 and restored it to its 1920s–30s heyday style. With the main building and two wings, the inn now has 88 rooms, a lounge, a restaurant, tennis courts, a pool, and a dock on the lake. Perhaps the most enjoyable activity though, is sitting in one of the rocking chairs on the main lodge's expansive veranda, sipping iced tea and soaking up the view across placid Lake Dora.

Mount Dora offers more intimate lodging as well. Two bed & breakfasts within easy walking distance of downtown are the Magnolia Inn Bed & Breakfast, with Victorian-decorated rooms and a carriage house in a 1926 mansion built by prominent Mount Dora newspaper owner and neighborhood developer L. R. Heim, and the Adora Inn Bed & Breakfast, an artfully restored three-story 1916 bungalow with an interior that cleverly blends traditional arts and crafts with 1950s modern style.

One of the most historic and ornate houses in Mount Dora is the Donnelly House at the uphill end of Donnelly Street between Fifth and Sixth avenues. The Masonic Lodge currently owns it, meaning entry's limited to special events, but the outside is a grand example of Queen Anne Victorian style. In Donnelly's day—the late 1800s to early 1900s—it was referred to as the "gingerbread house." Donnelly had homesteaded 160 acres adjacent to property owned by Annie Stone, one of the earliest homesteaders. In 1881, the two married and began the development of what is now downtown Mount Dora. They built their gingerbread house in 1893. Donnelly, one of Mount Dora's most prominent citizens, went on to be the town's first mayor in 1910. In 1924, he sold the large tract of land across the street from his house to the city for a park named in honor of his wife.

Mount Dora has long been a popular destination for antique shoppers, but the town is also known for its unusual shops. One such place is Thee Clockmaker's Shoppe in the old Simpson Hotel Building, where owner Roy Gress sells and repairs antique and new grandfather and grandmother (they're shorter) clocks. And pet lovers love to visit Piglet's Pantry Dog Bakery, which bakes "to slobber for" doggie treats and carries a great selection of gifts and toys for both dogs and cats, as well as for their owners.

Thee Clockmaker's Shoppe

Mount Dora has a terrific selection of fine restaurants worth checking out. The Goblin Market Restaurant is a hidden culinary jewel nestled into a pedestrian alley. It may sound odd to get excited about soup, but theirs is amazing. Try the Irish whiskey onion soup or the crab bisque. Then choose from delectable entrées like New Zealand rack of lamb encrusted with fennel, mustard seed, and roasted garlic, topped with a brandy mint demi-glace; and wasabi-crusted salmon with a honey butter and soy glaze. At the Windsor Rose English Tea Room, the menu features "spot on" traditional British fare such as cottage pie and bangers and mash. Fresh seafood with a view of Lake Dora is the prime attraction at Pisces Rising, along with an atmosphere and menu that crosses Key West with Bourbon Street (great shrimp and grits). The Gables Restaurant's picturesque garden setting, great selection of lunch salads (like Elaine's chicken salad with pineapples, grapes, and apples), and wide variety of dinner entrées (coconut-crusted grouper, vegetarian lasagna, chicken primavera), make it one of Mount Dora's most popular eateries.

Mount Dora is easily explored on foot, but if your legs get tired, you can rent a Segway at Segway of Central Florida, right in downtown.

DIRECTIONS: From Orlando to Mount Dora (29 miles), take US Highway 441 north.

DON'T MISS: The Goblin Market Restaurant

LAKE WALES

Population: 14,245

FROM MY CHILDHOOD DAYS in Tampa in the 1960s, my only recollection about Lake Wales was Spook Hill. Supposedly, the hill was home to some bizarre gravitational anomaly that was strong enough to pull a car uphill. Indeed, when we visited the spot and put the family Oldsmobile in neutral, it did seem to roll uphill. Sometime back in the 1950s, the city recognized a good tourist draw when they saw one and put up a sign about "The Legend of Spook Hill," which was something about an Indian chief and his nemesis, a giant alligator. It's not really clear, however, what the connection was supposed to be between the Indian chief and cars rolling uphill.

Lake Wales was founded in 1911 by four investors–G. V. Tillman, C. L. Johnson, B. K. Bullard, and E. C. Stuart–who formed the Lake

Wales Land Company. Tillman and Johnson had come from the naval supply industry and saw good potential here for turpentine and lumber harvesting, all in a scenic region that could attract settlers, and therefore a workforce. By 1917 the town had incorporated, and in 1921 it received its municipal charter.

An unexpected boon came to Lake Wales the following year when Edward Bok purchased fifteen acres just north of town, on top of a ridge that locals called Iron Mountain. His plan was to build a park.

Edward William Bok had immigrated to the United States from Holland with his family in 1869, when he was six years old. He grew up in New York and went into the publishing business. By 1889 he had worked his way up to editor of *Ladies Home Journal*. He also wrote his autobiography, *The Americanization of Edward Bok*, which won him a Pulitzer Prize in 1920. After retiring from *Ladies Home Journal*, he devoted his time to various worthy causes, including the establishment of the American Peace Award.

In 1923, Bok hired famous landscape architect Frederick Law Olmstead Jr. to design his park and bird sanctuary. Olmstead brought in a colorful assortment of trees, flowers, and plants that would be viable in Florida's fertile climate. He built duck ponds and set more than fifty birdbaths along paths that meander through the gardens. Bok even imported nightingales from England because he loved their singing. Although the gardens turned out to be everything Bok had envisioned, he felt that they still needed a centerpiece. He decided on a carillon tower, and commissioned architect Milton B. Medary to design one, with the 400-year-old carillon tower in Mechlin, Belgium, as his inspiration. Medary and Olmstead worked together to refocus the park on the site chosen for the tower. Construction took another two years, but the result was a 205-foot-tall Gothic marble and coquina rock masterpiece with 71 bells (now pared down to 60) housed in the 40-foot-tall bell chamber.

Carvings on the tower depict Florida native birds—herons, cranes, swans, eagles, pelicans, and flamingos—and Florida trees and plants. One outstanding feature is the nine-and-a-half-foot-tall sundial on the tower's south-facing wall. It includes President Calvin Coolidge's February 1, 1929, dedication of the tower, which reads: "This singing tower with its adjacent sanctuary was dedicated and presented for visitation to the American people by Calvin Coolidge, President of the United States." The north side of the tower is mirrored in a long reflecting pond that extends out from its base. The only entryway into the tower is through a magnificent brass-overlaid teakwood door on its north side. Unfortunately, the interior is not open to the public.

Today, Bok Tower Gardens is, in my opinion, Florida's most beautiful and idyllic spot. Bok considered the gardens his gift to the American people in gratitude for the opportunity that they had afforded him; he hoped the park would be "a spot which would reach out in its beauty through the architecture of the tower, through the music of the carillon, to the people, and fill their souls with the quiet, the repose, the influence of the beautiful, as they could see it and enjoy it in these gardens and through this tower." He died in 1930, only a year after its dedication, but he passed away within sight of the tower and within earshot of his carillon.

In 1990, Lake Wales' downtown commercial district, which has significant architecture from the 1920s, was recognized as a National Historic District. Among many renovated downtown buildings is the ornate Mediterranean-style Rhodesbilt Arcade building in the center of downtown. Real estate investor and building contractor Jesse Rhodes built it in 1924. The building's open arcade runs the entire block between Park Avenue and Stuart Avenue. Others include the Bullard Building on Stuart Avenue, built by city co-founder B. K. Bullard in 1919, and the Atlantic Coast Line Railroad Depot, originally built in 1928 and renovated in 1976 as the Lake Wales Museum & Cultural Center. One of the most interesting buildings in Lake Wales is the Dixie Walesbilt Grand Hotel on North 1st Street, built in 1927. At ten stories, it was a skyscraper by 1920s standards. Currently the hotel is empty and has not been renovated.

The historic designation has generated a revival of downtown business, including some very good restaurants. Coqui Taino, in the Rhodesbilt Arcade building, is an outstanding family-run authentic Puerto Rican restaurant. For fine French dining, try Très Jolie on Park Avenue. It has a great bakery too.

Also, perhaps taking a cue from Lake Placid, the city has started a mural project, with giant murals on the sides of downtown buildings depicting historic Lake Wales events and people.

Stuart Avenue

Besides Bok Tower and Spook Hill, Lake Wales has long been famous for an unusual inn and restaurant just north of town. In the 1920s, Carl and Bertha Hinshaw had plans to develop a golf community in the rolling countryside near Lake Wales. Kraft Cheese Company president J. L. Kraft was to be a major partner, but timing worked against them. The collapse of the Florida real estate market and the stock market crash of 1929 brought the project to a grinding halt. Then, in 1931, Carl, just forty-seven years old, passed away from severe pneumonia. Bertha, left with two young children, Carl Jr. and Suzanne, was determined to find a way to provide for her family. That same year she opened Suzanne's Tavern (named for her daughter). Soon she changed the name to Suzanne's Chalet, and then later to Chalet Suzanne.

Duncan Hines (yes, the cake-baking Duncan Hines), an early patron, helped put Chalet Suzanne on the map when he included it in his 1930s book *Adventures in Good Eating.*

In the 1940s, a fire leveled the Chalet. Upon his return from World War II, Carl Jr. helped his mother rebuild it using whatever materials and resources they had at their disposal. They relocated several buildings, including part of a horse stable and a chicken house, to construct what would eventually evolve into today's dining hall that overlooks Lake Suzanne.

Chalet Suzanne, still run by the Hinshaw family, is unlike any inn I've ever visited. Actually, it is more like a fairytale village than an inn. The grounds spread across seventy acres. Rambling brick walkways meander past fountains, gardens, and courtyards, and wind through the colorful village, where each of the rooms (no two alike) has its own entrance. A tiny antiques shop/museum and a ceramics shop are nestled at the east end. The restaurant overlooks the lake to the north and the Chalet's own private 2,500-foot grass airstrip to the west. Private pilots from around the state have been flying in to the Chalet Suzanne for dinner for many years.

Dinner at Chalet Suzanne's restaurant is a six-course, all-evening affair, and is quite elegant (as well as quite expensive). The restaurant's gourmet meals are known worldwide, but it is perhaps most famous for its soups. The owners began canning their own soups in 1956. In 1973, NASA sent cans of Chalet Suzanne's Romaine soup to the moon on Apollo 15, as part of the astronaut's food supply. The "Moon Soup" has been on several missions since.

DIRECTIONS: From Tampa, go east on State Road 60 (59 miles to Lake Wales). To get to Bok Tower Gardens, turn north on Highway 27, then east on Mountain Lake Cut-off Road and follow the signs.

DON'T MISS: Bok Tower

INVERNESS

Population: 7,151

*T*HE ROUGH-AND-READY Tompkins brothers, Civil War veterans who had fought for the Confederacy, settled here in 1868. They called it Tompkinsville. Records show that the name changed to Inverness in 1889. Local legend claims that an emigrant Scotsman (whose name no one knows anymore) became homesick while standing on the banks of Lake Tsala Apopka (adjacent to Tompkinsville/ Inverness). It reminded him of the lake country near his home in Inverness, Scotland. At least one report claims that the Scotsman was one of the many phosphate-boom speculators who swarmed to north-central Florida in the late 1880s and early 1890s and that he offered to donate two thousand dollars toward the construction of a new courthouse if the name of the town was changed.

In 1887, the newly formed Citrus County had designated the nearby town of Mannfield as the temporary county seat. Four years later, a county election decided that Inverness would become the permanent county seat—much to the disappointment of the residents of Mannfield and to the consternation of Senator Austin S. Mann, who developed Mannfield. W. C. Zimmerman, clerk of the circuit court at that time, refused to vacate the old Mannfield office, and refused to deliver the county records to the new location. He actually sat at his desk while the entire office was removed from around him and loaded onto a wagon. Finally, the sheriff and a contingent of deputies loaded Zimmerman, still in his chair, onto the wagon along with his desk and boxes of records and transported everything to the new offices in Inverness. Accounts I have read say that Zimmerman continued to record minutes throughout the trip. Inverness went on to become a center of commerce while Mannfield became a ghost town. Zimmerman later became the Citrus County superintendent of schools.

At first, Inverness townsfolk feared that the widening of US Highway 41 in 1993, and the consequential bypass of their downtown Main Street, would be the equivalent of cutting off the blood supply to a limb. Happily, the opposite happened. Thanks to a committee of local business people, instead of succumbing to a withering death, downtown Inverness got an injection of new life. Its one-block-long Main Street—the historic Citrus County Courthouse marking its east end and the twenty-foot-tall Bank of Inverness clock at its west end—is now a vibrant district with restaurants, galleries, and shops.

Today gas lantern–style street lights blend well with Main Street's restored buildings and storefronts. The brick, three-story, neoclassical-revival Masonic Lodge Building at the corner of Main and Pine Streets was considered a skyscraper when it was constructed (for $17,285) in 1910. The Masons leased the first floor to retail shops and the second floor to a dance and theater production group, using the third floor as their lodge. These days the restored building once again has retail shops downstairs. The Citrus County Board of County Commissioners, a real estate office, and a law firm occupy the upper floors.

The old yellow-brick 1912 Citrus County Courthouse, which replaced the original 1892 wood structure, has been immaculately restored under the supervision of the Citrus County Historical Society. The process, completed in October 2000, took eight years and $2.5 million. It is now home to the Old Courthouse Heritage Museum. Downstairs, rooms that previously housed the offices of tax collectors, judges, and clerks of the court are now galleries portraying local history, exhibits of pre- and early-history artifacts, and one room is now the museum store. The most impressive room, however, is the old courtroom, which occupies the entire second floor. Architects used old photographs to accurately reconstruct details throughout the building, but for the courtroom they watched old reels of the 1961 Elvis Presley movie *Follow That Dream.* The closing scene for the movie was filmed in the second-floor courtroom and was the best historical record of what the room looked like then. (Much of the movie was also filmed in Yankeetown. For more information, see the Yankeetown chapter.)

Many of Inverness' other buildings and houses from its prosperous turn-of-the-century era are still in use. Some have been restored. One of the most impeccable restorations is the Citrus High School, now the administration building for Citrus Memorial Hospital. This red-brick, two-story building with a bell tower over its entrance was originally built in 1911 and restored in 1992.

Main Street and 1912 Citrus County Courthouse

Another interesting historic home is the 1900 Hicks House, at the corner of Tompkins Street and Osceola Avenue. Robert Hicks designed and built this unusual octagonal-shaped house to withstand hurricanes. It is still in the Hicks family today, and may be the oldest home in Inverness.

Perhaps Inverness' most recognizable historic building is the Crown Hotel. This grand three-story wooden hotel building had much more humble beginnings. The Crown began life as a general store when Alf, one of the Tompkins brothers, gave his brother-in-law, Francis Dampier, property on which to build a store. Dampier built the store on one side of the street and his home on the other side. Sometime around 1900, Dampier moved his store from Bay Street to Main Street, and in 1907 he turned it into a boarding house called the Orange Hotel. Ten years after that, he sold it to a New York hotel syndicate, which moved it again in 1926, this time around the corner to Seminole Avenue, its present location.

In conjunction with the move, the New York group performed what must have been an amazing feat of construction in its day: They built an entirely new bottom floor, then hoisted the original two-story building up into the air and placed it on top of the new first floor to make a three-story hotel, which they named the Colonial.

The Colonial was a popular place for a number of decades, but by the 1970s it had fallen into serious disrepair. It had recently been condemned when, in 1979, the British company Epicure Holdings purchased it and spent $2 million renovating it into the decidedly British Crown Hotel. At one time, the hotel even had its own authentic 1909 double-decker bus, purchased at an auction in London. It was an Inverness landmark that sat parked in front of the Crown for many years. The hotel was sold to Nigel and Jill Sumner in 1990, and then sold again in 2001, when it was converted into an assisted living facility, The Crown Court, which it remains today.

Bicycle touring has become very popular in and around Inverness. The forty-six-mile-long Withlacoochee State Trail (which runs roughly from Trilby in the south to Dunnellon in the north) was one of Florida's first Rails-to-Trails projects, and is its longest paved rail-trail. The state bought the rail right-of-way, which was no longer in use, and converted it into a state park trail. It comes to its approximate two-thirds point in Inverness and passes through just a couple of blocks north of downtown.

There's plenty to eat at Inverness' Main Street restaurants. Head to Stumpknocker's for seafood, frog legs, and gator tail; Coach's Pub & Eatery for burgers and wings; and Angelo's Pizzeria for outstanding pizza.

DIRECTIONS: Take US Highway 41 north from Brooksville.

DON'T MISS: The Old Courthouse Heritage Museum

FLORAL CITY, PINEOLA, ISTACHATTA, NOBLETON

Population: Floral City 4,989; Pineola 50; Istachatta 93; Nobleton 50

*A*LL WHO DRIVE DOWN ORANGE AVENUE in Floral City for the first time have to stop and marvel at the grand oaks that reach clear across the road to intertwine with one another. Over the past one hundred thirty years, those trees have grown tall and wide, crossing over the top of the road and forming a quarter-mile-long tunnel known as the "Avenue of Oaks."

Aroostook Avenue, with its own rows of oak trees, forks diagonally northeast from Orange Avenue and dead-ends at the shore of Lake Tsala Apopka. This was a busy steamboat port from which oranges, along with lumber and the occasional passenger, could be shipped via the newly completed (in 1884) Orange State Canal down the

Withlacoochee River to the railhead at Lake Panasoffkee. Aroostook Avenue was Floral City's original Main Street until the big freeze of 1894–95 killed the area's citrus industry and ended the steamboat business. Fortunately, right around the same time, phosphate was discovered nearby. Mines opened up, and Floral City had a new industry.

The picturesque town of Floral City, established in 1884, has an impressive collection of historic homes and buildings. Some are restored but most are simply well preserved. Many were built during the phosphate boom (1890s–1910s), when Floral City's population swelled briefly to over ten thousand with the influx of transient mine workers. At least one house predates that era: The Formy-Duval House, at 7801 Old Floral City Road (which runs north and south a couple of blocks east of Highway 41), built in 1865. It is the oldest house still standing in the area. John Paul Formy-Duval was a cotton, sugarcane, and citrus farmer who owned vast tracts of land surrounding the southern end of Lake Tsala Apopka. Some of his land, 342 acres, would eventually become the town of Floral City.

The 1894 D. A. Tooke House, at 8560 Orange Avenue, and the 1910 J. T. Love House, next door at 8580 Orange Avenue, are two good examples of Queen Anne Victorian architectural style. Both are large one-story homes with twin, steep-roofed gables. The simple wood-frame Floral City Methodist Church, at 8508 Marvin Street (a block north of Orange Avenue), has been in continuous use since its construction in 1884. The Cracker Victorian–style W. C. Zimmerman House, at 8441 East Orange Avenue, was built in 1890. (See the Inverness chapter for more about W. C. Zimmerman.) The cedar shingle–sided Soloman Moon House, at 8860 East Orange Avenue, was built in 1893. The 1904 William H. Dunn House, at 8050 South Bedford Road (on the west side of Highway 41 and several blocks south of Orange Avenue), is the boyhood home of well-known Florida historian Hampton Dunn.

The two-story 1889 Commercial Hotel (also called the Magnolia Hotel) at 8375 East Orange Avenue—with its full-width front porch, leaded stained-glass windows, and triple-gabled roof—was originally the home of James Baker, son-in-law of town developer John Paul Formy-Duval. The house was relocated from two blocks away in 1895 and converted into an elegant hotel. It is now a private residence.

Floral City's largest business is citrus grower Ferris Groves. Doc Ferris started his orange grove business in 1927, when he took over property on Duval Island (in Lake Tsala Apopka), on which his father had originally intended to build a golf course. Ferris reintroduced citrus to the area after its forty-year absence. In 1940, Ferris built a packing plant and a roadside fruit stand on Highway 41 just north of Orange Avenue. In 1955, he built a permanent fruit store and gift shop that still operates today. It is reminiscent of the many tourist shops that sprang up in the 1950s and '60s along Florida thoroughfares. After another hard freeze in the mid-1980s, the folks at Ferris Groves changed their focus to strawberries, for which they are famous today.

A bit of Floral City trivia: A few of the town's residents were relatives of famous people. Doc Ferris was the grandnephew of George Washington Gale Ferris, who invented the Ferris wheel and introduced it at the 1893 Chicago World's Fair. One of Floral City's early (1880s) orange grove farmers, Jacob Clemens, was the cousin of Samuel Clemens (Mark Twain). Floral City resident Robert Dillinger (by all accounts, a mild-mannered fellow) was cousin to notorious 1930s gangster John Dillinger. Floral City's best-known native was Hampton Dunn, a longtime Tampa resident. When Mr. Dunn passed away in February 2002, Florida lost one of its finest historians (and one of my favorite Florida history resources). No one could bring Florida's past to life like Hampton Dunn.

The Heritage Hall Museum and Country Store opened in 2009 in the old fire station building on Orange Avenue. The museum features displays of historic photographs and maps as well as dioramas that chronicle the history of Floral City and the surrounding region.

While this is a book about small towns, once in a while the roads that run between them merit mentioning. That is the case with Istachatta Road (CR 39) heading south out of Floral City. It is one of my favorite top-down roadster roads, winding over scenic rolling hills, through oak hammocks, and past horse farms and pastureland for seven miles. It parallels and crisscrosses the Withlacoochee State Trail. Near its south end, it eases into quiet Pineola, made up of a handful of residences and an old cemetery next to the New Hope United Methodist Church, one of the oldest churches in this area.

Istachatta General Store

Church founders built the original New Hope Church out of logs on this site in 1830, and then replaced it with a wood-frame structure following a fire in 1886. In 1940, the congregation built the current church, reusing much of the lumber from the 1886 building. Some of the hand-hewn pews are from the original 1830 church. New Hope's annual October Homecoming draws a good-size crowd of past parishioners from around the state.

Just past Pineola is Istachatta. The name has been variously interpreted as Creek Indian for "red man" and "man's river crossing." There was a ferry crossing here on the Withlacoochee River in the 1800s that was replaced by an iron bridge in 1910 (which is no longer there). Istachatta has a community park, a library, a tiny post office, and the Istachatta General Store. This is a real general store, not one done up for tourists. The shelves are filled with staples—canned goods, flour, butter, milk, and eggs. A handwritten sign on the wall reads, "Boiled Peanuts $1.99 a Qt." Sometimes they have live music on Friday nights. The store also has three tables, and serves breakfast and lunch. I'm kind of partial to the cheeseburger.

Continuing south, then east, on Lake Lindsey Road (CR 476) for about a mile and a half brings you to Nobleton, at the crossing of the Withlacoochee River. The Nobleton Boat Rental Outpost, on the north side of the highway, rents canoes, kayaks, and pontoon boats, and also offers airboat rides.

These four communities still retain much of their old-Florida flavor, and I hope that never changes.

DIRECTIONS: **Floral City**: Take US Highway 41, 16 miles north of Brooksville, or 7 miles south of Inverness.
Pineola and **Istachatta**: From Floral City, take CR 48 (Orange Avenue) east to CR 39 (Istachatta Road) and go south.
Nobleton: Take CR 476, east of CR 39.

DON'T MISS: Floral City Heritage Hall Museum and Country Store

ARIPEKA, BAYPORT, CHASSAHOWITZKA, OZELLO

Population: Aripeka 200; Bayport 36; Chassahowitzka 300; Ozello 300

*U*S HIGHWAY 19, from Clearwater north to Hudson, is one of the most heavily trafficked roads in central Florida. But five miles farther north, turn west down Pasco County Road 595/ Aripeka Road and the scenery changes dramatically. Pastureland replaces parking lots, and then gives way to piney woods and brackish swamps as you approach the small, coastal port community of Aripeka.

Aripeka was called Gulf Key when it was first settled in 1886. Back then, visitors rode the *Governor Stafford* passenger steamer here for fishing and recreation. They stayed at the Osawaw Inn (now gone), built by the Aripeka Saw Mill Company. Gulf Key adopted its new name from the company. Aripeka is most likely a slight variation on Arpeika, a Miccosukee-Seminole chief who also went by the name of Sam Jones. In 1835, just prior to the Second Seminole War, then-governor Andrew Jackson mandated that all Seminole Indians be removed from Florida and sent to reservations out West. Chief Arpeika was one of eight tribe leaders who refused to relocate his people. Instead, they fled south to the Everglades and established Sam Jones Old Town near present-day Fort Lauderdale. An alternate claim is that Aripeka is a mispronunciation of another Seminole leader's name, Apayaka.

Thankfully, Aripeka's rate of growth has been nominal over the past century. It is still a quiet fishing enclave. A few stilt fishing shacks appear alongside the road as it slows at a sharp S-turn before bridging the south fork and then the north fork of Hammock Creek. The small Norfleet's Bait and Tackle general store sits between the bridges and backs up to Hammock Creek. It's been here since the 1930s and today is run by second-generation owner Carl Norfleet. The faded wooden sign on the front depicts a palm tree, beach, and sunset paradise. It reads "Aripeka, Fla. 5.9 miles from Heaven." Inside, fishing lures, leaders, rod-and-reels, bait buckets, and long-billed hats hang on racks and occupy shelves alongside groceries. On one of my visits I asked Carl Norfleet, "What is it that's five point nine miles away?" He replied, "Five point nine miles to the best fishing spot in the Gulf, but I'm not saying in which direction." This is the heart of Aripeka. No motels. No restaurants. Just a quiet place to cast a net or drop a line and soak up the idyllic scenery. From here west, Hammock Creek spills out across a saw grass delta and into the Gulf of Mexico. If Heaven is 5.9 miles out there somewhere, then Aripeka must be the Pearly Gates.

CR 595 continues north from Aripeka and follows the shoreline for a couple of miles. It's difficult to tell where the saw grass ends and the Gulf begins. Turn west on Highway 50, which leads to Bayport on a marshy point at the mouth of the Weeki Wachee River. The road ends at a picturesque park with a boat ramp.

Bayport was a lumber, cotton, and supplies port during the Civil War. Like many other small Gulf Coast ports, Bayport became

Norfleet's Bait and Tackle Store

vital after the Union's East Gulf Blockading Squadron succeeded in cutting off the larger ports. By 1864, Union troops felt that Bayport had become significant enough to warrant invasion too. For twenty years after the war ended, Bayport was a bustling town and the area's busiest port. Regularly scheduled wagon runs transported goods between here and Brooksville. But in 1885, rail service came to Brooksville, and Bayport's usefulness declined rapidly. Nothing remains of the town today, but the boat ramp at Bayport Park is a popular put-in spot for the Weeki Wachee River.

Back out on US 19, continue north and pass DOT signs that warn drivers to watch for bears crossing. This is one of the few remaining habitats for Florida black bears. Just north of the Hernando-Citrus county line, Miss Maggie Road turns west off of US 19 and winds down to Chassahowitzka (Timucuan Indian for "pumpkin place"). It ends at the Chassahowitzka River Campground and Recreational Area, the best place to rent canoes or kayaks to explore the Chassahowitzka National Wildlife Refuge. The Refuge encompasses more than thirty

Bayport Park

thousand acres of brackish marsh and salt bays, stretching from Raccoon Point north to the mouth of the Homosassa River. It is home to several hundred species of birds, including a variety of herons, pelicans, ducks, ospreys, and even bald eagles. Manatees, green sea turtles, deer, and a small population of black bears live here as well.

Overnighters should consider the Chassahowitzka Hotel, just up the road. David and Kim Strickland opened the current version in 2000, but it was David's grandparents, Ben and Eliza Smith, who built the original on this same site in 1910.

Just north of Homosassa, turn west on Citrus County 494/West Ozello Trail. For a mile or so, the road winds through a swampy forest. There's no shoulder. The palmetto scrub grows wild right up to the edge of the road. As you near the coast, the road intermittently opens up to saw grass savannas dotted with cedar bay heads. The community of Ozello (the westernmost in Citrus County) is technically on an island, separated from the mainland by tributaries

Peck's Old Port Cove Seafood Restaurant

of the St. Martin River, Salt Creek, and Greenleaf Bay. Hundreds of water passageways crosshatch this nether land, looking like varicose veins on the map. Airboats are the transport of choice here.

Until 1955, Ozello Trail was an oyster-shell path with palmetto logs bridging the swampy sections. It frequently flooded out, but this was no deterrent to the local residents, who were accustomed to getting around by boat. From 1880 until 1943, Ozello's children daily paddled rowboats and canoes to their one-room schoolhouse on one of the many tiny hammocks in the bay just south of Ozello. They called it the Isle of Knowledge. The island is still there (south off the end of John Brown Road), but unfortunately the schoolhouse is gone.

Ozello Trail ends at the edge of the open Gulf of Mexico and at Peck's Old Port Cove Seafood Restaurant and Blue Crab Farm. Calvin Peck began harvesting blue crabs in specially constructed tanks behind his restaurant in 1982. Around back, you can survey the operation. Hundreds of blue crabs fill fourteen tanks. On my first visit to Peck's, back in 1998, I devoured a heaping, steaming plate of garlic crabs. The last time I stopped in, I tried to exercise more culinary restraint and just ordered the fried grouper fingers, with coleslaw, fries, and the requisite hush puppies—fresh and delicious as always.

DIRECTIONS: **Aripeka**: Five miles north of Hudson, take CR 595 west off US 19 to Aripeka.

Chassahowitzka: Go west on Miss Maggie Drive off US 19, just north of the Citrus/Hernando County line.

Bayport: Continue north from Aripeka on CR 595 to Highway 50 and go west to Bayport.

Ozello: Go west on Citrus County 494/West Ozello Trail off US 19 between Homosassa and Crystal River to Ozello.

DON'T MISS: Peck's Old Port Cove Seafood Restaurant

WEBSTER

Population: 911

*E*very Monday, the Sumter County Farmers Market in Webster hosts Florida's largest and probably oldest flea market. Sumter County has always had an agriculture-based economy. Citrus was big here prior to the Great Freeze of 1894. After that, peppers, cucumbers, cabbage, lettuce, beans, and other vegetables became the staple crops. In the early 1900s, Webster was known as the "Cucumber Capital." In 1937, a group of local farmers formed a co-op and, without state funding or financial help from the county, built a market in the middle of Webster from which to auction their produce. The farmers built the facility themselves, harvesting cypress trees from nearby swamp lands and using mules to drag out the lumber. The farmers

Fresh fruit and vegetables at Webster Flea Market

market was then and remains today a not-for-profit operation. It is still owned and operated by local agricultural business people.

Over the decades, the market evolved along with changes in local farming trends. A cattle auction (now the second largest in Florida) replaced the vegetable auction, and people began to sell other items out of the empty produce stalls. Every week, fifty-two weeks a year, the cattle auction takes place on Tuesdays, and the flea market on Mondays—at least, unless Christmas comes on a Monday or Tuesday.

The forty-acre facility can seem overwhelming to first-time visitors. A dozen roofed, open-air walkways with hundreds of vendor stalls, plus several more enclosed buildings and open paved lots, house more than fifteen hundred vendors, who contract for their spaces on an annual basis. Except for occasional cancellations, there are no vacancies. Each space has been booked for years. This is a busy place with a carnival-like atmosphere. The market opens at 6:30 A.M. and closes at 4 P.M., and there's a crowd here most of the day. A sign at the entrance reads "No trespassing, except on Mondays."

They sell everything here, some of it new but most of it used. One person's discards are another's treasure—antiques, computer equipment, hunting knives, power tools, parakeets, flowers, jewelry, watches, musical instruments, golf clubs, grandfather clocks, comic books, old records, Barbie dolls (and all accessories), Matchbox cars, sports trading cards, coins, and stamps. If someone collects it, there's a vendor for it here. There are clothes and whole bolts of fabric, bicycles and baby carriages, Nintendo games and stuffed teddy bears.

One of the most popular sections features rows of stalls filled with fresh fruits and vegetables: peaches, plums, pears, peppers, squash, nectarines, tomatoes, onions. A wonderful fresh aroma floats up and down these aisles. Speaking of food, they don't want you to go hungry, so concessionaires sell the usual assortment of corn dogs, curly fries, and Italian sausage sandwiches, as well as tantalizing sweets like caramelized cinnamon-roasted pecans.

DIRECTIONS: Take the Highway 50 (Brooksville) exit east from I-75 to Highway 471, then head north.

DON'T MISS: The Sumter County Farmers Market flea market (Remember: Mondays only)

TRILBY, LACOOCHEE

Population: Trilby 200; Lacoochee 1,345

*A*BOUT SEVEN MILES NORTH of Dade City, there is a state road sign that reads "Trilacoochee." I wonder, was the state trying to save money by combining "Trilby" and "Lacoochee" into one name on one sign? Granted, these two tiny communities are right next to each other, but they are separate communities. Just west of Highway 301 lies tiny Trilby, at the crossing of Highway 98 and CR 575, where you will find the historic "Little Brown Church of the South"—officially, the Trilby Methodist Church. Charter church members and Reverend T. H. Sistrunk built this wood-frame, tin-roof structure, with its tall steeple rising above the entranceway, in 1897 and 1898. Ninety years later it underwent some remodeling, but most of it—including the steeple outside, and the pulpit inside—is original. Next door, a historical marker explains that the 1870s settlement of McLeod changed its name to Macon in 1885 when the first post office opened. In 1896, the name changed again, this time to Trilby, after George du Maurier's popular novel of the same name. Town officials also named several of the streets and the town's Svengali Square after characters from the novel.

At one time, Trilby had a bank, a school, a railway station, two hotels, a sawmill, a grist mill, a grocery store, a dry goods store, a drug-and-sundries store with a soda fountain, and a tuberculosis hospital. In the 1920s, it was a busy little town. That all changed in one afternoon in May 1925. Townspeople first spotted smoke coming from the second floor of the dry goods store around 1 P.M. They quickly started a bucket brigade, taking water from the water tower at the south end of town. Dade City's fire truck rushed to the scene, but during the time it took to drive the eight miles, flames had consumed all of the buildings on the west side of the railroad tracks. By 5 P.M., firefighters had contained the blaze, but most of downtown Trilby was gone. Some was rebuilt, but the town never fully recovered from that tragic afternoon. Thankfully, one of the buildings left standing was the Little Brown Church of the South.

From Trilby, drive east on County Road 575, across Highway 301, and you'll come to Lacoochee. As was the case for so many Florida small towns, it was the railroad that planted the seeds of this settlement when it came through in the mid-1880s. The Lacoochee Post Office was established in 1888. In 1922, the Cummer Cypress Company came to log cypress from the nearby Lacoochee Swamp and built a sawmill here. Lacoochee was a company town until the mill closed in 1959.

Just south of Lacoochee is one of my Mom-and-Pop eatery finds, George and Gladys' Bar-B-Q. It hasn't changed one bit since it opened in 1957, and I suspect the various stuffed critters hanging on the walls have been here since then too. George and Gladys' ranks high on my list of favorite barbecue spots (and I eat a lot of barbecue). The chipped pork sandwich with a side of three-bean salad is my standard lunch here.

George and Gladys' Bar-B-Q

DIRECTIONS: Take Highway 301 north from Dade City, then take left fork at Highway 98 to go to Trilby, or turn east on CR 575 to go to Lacoochee.

DON'T MISS: The Little Brown Church of the South

DADE CITY

Population: 7,190

*T*WENTY-FIVE MILES NORTH OF TAMPA, the terrain
turns hilly as US Highway 301 rolls into Dade City. U.S. Army major Francis Dade and his troops camped near here in December 1835,
just days before meeting their demise at the Dade Massacre (near
Bushnell), which sparked the beginning of the Second Seminole War.

Today, Dade City is an antiques and knickknack shopper's
paradise, and most shops are within walking distance of the main
downtown intersection of 7th Street (Highway 301) and Meridian
Avenue. Sugar Creek Too Antiques and Church Street Antiques are
just a couple in the district. One of my favorites is The Picket Fence,
which specializes in teddy bears. It's located in the bright yellow 1927

S. J. Lewis bungalow, which was relocated to Meridian Avenue from 8th Street in 1995.

Each Labor Day weekend, Dade City holds its Pioneer Days Festival at the Pioneer Florida Museum on the north edge of town. When it opened in 1961, the museum displayed pioneer-era (1800s to early 1900s) farm implements and equipment that had been donated to the Pasco County Fair. Since then, the museum has expanded considerably, acquiring five pioneer-era buildings and relocating them to the museum grounds: the 1878 Enterprise Methodist Church; a shoe-repair shop built in 1913; the 1896 Trilby, Florida, train depot; a bright-red one-room schoolhouse from Lacoochee, Florida, built in 1926; and an 1860s farmhouse that belonged to John Overstreet, who built it from native heart pine cut with a steam-operated band saw and hand tools on his eighty-acre homestead farm near here. As was customary in those days, the kitchen was a separate building behind the house that was connected by a covered walkway. That way, if a fire started in the kitchen, it was less likely to burn down the whole house.

The museum's main building has on display many locally found pioneer artifacts, but it also houses some much older items. One display case features an impressive collection of archaic arrowheads, some dating back to 5000-3000 BC.

Pioneer Museum

There are two great lunch spots in Dade City. The first is Lunch on Limoges on 7th Street, owned and run by Skip Mize and Phil Williams. Phil is the third generation of Williamses to operate what began as Williams Department Store in 1908. Lunch tables blend right into a boutique shop on one side of the large room. The black-and-white checkerboard floor and tall ceilings echo the busy sounds of the open kitchen, which Skip built. They serve what I can best describe as Southern-gourmet fare. The chalkboard menu changes daily plus there are a few regular items. One of their best is the pecan grouper. The second lunch spot I enjoy is Mallie Kyla's Café, which opened on Meridian Avenue in Dade City in 1996 and later moved to the American Eagle Antique Mall just around the corner on 7th Street. Mallie Kyla's is famous for their pies and cakes—try the red velvet cake.

DIRECTIONS: Take Highway 301 north from Tampa. Continue north through Zephyrhills.

DON'T MISS: The Pioneer Florida Museum

CHRISTMAS

Population: 1,162

O<small>N THE COUNTER</small> at the post office in Christmas, Florida, there's a green ink pad and a box filled with rubber stamps to commemorate an assortment of holidays and special occasions. Patrons are encouraged to adorn their envelopes with the stamps.

I asked a counter worker named Rose once if things get hectic here right before Christmas. "Hectic?" She replied. "Yes, but it's a wonderful time. The only people who come all the way to Christmas, Florida, just to mail their cards and packages are people who really love other people. Why else would they go through that much trouble just to have Christmas on their postmark?"

Not only do people come by in person, but starting in November of each year, the Christmas Post Office begins receiving boxes of letters and packages to mail out with the Christmas postmark. This small post office becomes a busy clearinghouse for parcels coming in from around the world and then going back out around the world, often right back to where they came from.

The Christmas postmark looks pretty much like any other: an oval with "Christmas, Florida" across the top, the date in the middle, and the 32709 zip code across the bottom. Each year, this little post office stamps and mails out over three hundred thousand Christmas cards, quite a bit for an office that serves an area with a population of fewer than twelve hundred. "It starts to get crazy the day after Thanksgiving, but we love it," says Rose.

The current Christmas Post Office was built in 1987. Paintings on the wall depict the 1918 and 1937 post office buildings. The first post office here was established in 1892 in the home of postmaster Samuel Hurlbut. His son Van delivered the mail twice a week on foot to as far away as Chuluota, twelve miles to the north.

Christmas was originally Fort Christmas. In only two days, United States Army troops under the command of General Abraham Eustis built the eighty-foot-by-eighty-foot log fort with two blockhouses. They began construction on December 25, 1837—hence the name. One of many forts built during the Second Seminole War (1835–42), Fort Christmas no longer stands, but there is an impressive re-creation, built in 1977, at the Fort Christmas Historical Park on Fort Christmas Road, two miles north of SR 50.

DIRECTIONS: Take SR 50 east from Orlando or west from Titusville.

DON'T MISS: Getting your Christmas cards stamped at the post office

YEEHAW JUNCTION

Population: 500

*N*O BOOK ABOUT SMALL TOWNS in Florida would be complete without mentioning Yeehaw Junction. The unusual name gets everyone's attention. Some say it is the more socially acceptable version of its original name, Jackass (that's the four-legged, floppy-eared variety) Crossing. Jackasses hauled lumber to railroad loading depots in the early 1900s, and this was a major crossing on their route. Yeehaw mimics the sound a jackass makes. Others contend that the name is a variation on the Creek Indian word *yaha*, meaning "wolf."

Truck drivers and traveling salesmen in the 1940s and 1950s knew Yeehaw Junction as the intersection of two of Florida's major thoroughfares, Highway 441 and State Road 60. The Desert Inn at the intersection's northwest corner was their standard stop for fuel, food, and a night's rest. According to some, they might also find a night's illicit entertainment. George and Stephanie Zicheck bought the old inn in 1986 from the estate of Fred and Julia Cheverette, who had owned it for forty years. The Zichecks' daughter Beverly began operating it the following year.

"My parents had homes in Tampa and West Palm Beach, and Yeehaw Junction is midway between the two, so we passed by here a lot," Beverly explained to me when I visited in 1996. "They bought the inn in nineteen eighty-six. When I first started operating it in February nineteen eighty-seven, everyone who came through the door would tell me, 'Please leave it like it's always been. Don't change anything.'" A 1950s Desert Inn postcard, hanging on the wall, was proof positive that the place does look exactly as it did back then. And the historic marker out front confirmed that Beverly intended to keep it that way. "When they passed the new commercial driver's license laws, business took a dive because the truckers couldn't buy beer and liquor at the package store anymore," she explained. "I needed something to revitalize interest in the place, and that's when I decided to start working on getting the Desert Inn included on the National Register of Historic Places. I can assure you that that's not something that happens easily. It was a lot of work."

During the first six months of her endeavor, she waded through Tallahassee's bureaucratic pea soup. First they sent her the wrong forms. Then they sent someone down to Yeehaw to help her, but that person was promptly transferred to another department. Finally, out of frustration, Beverly called Florida State Representative Bud Bronson. Within a week she received all the correct paperwork. Then she began the task of piecing together the Desert Inn's history. Through her contacts with several historical societies, she met Lucille Wright Sturgis, a writer who had done National Register projects before. Beverly and Lucille dug through libraries and court records, and they interviewed people who had lived and worked in this area as far back as the 1920s. The Desert Inn was finally placed on the National Register in January 1994.

The dining room and bar end of the inn sits close to the apex of the intersection of highways 441 and 60. The sound of air brakes and rumbling diesels is a constant background noise. Inside, the dozen or so tables and booths are arranged around the U-shaped bar. An old Wurlitzer jukebox plays mostly country classics—George Jones, Elvis Presley. Beverly collected some strange Florida memorabilia: plaques with clever sayings, stuffed jackalopes, rattlesnake hides, and other oddball knickknacks, many with a "jackass" motif. They're all hanging on the walls or displayed on shelves or on the bar. Two lifelike wooden Indians permanently occupy one corner table.

Although Yeehaw Junction might not be a place where you would spend an entire vacation, you should stop by the Desert Inn if you are passing through. In 2008, Beverly considered putting the inn up for sale, but ended up leasing it out instead. The new operators have kept the atmosphere the same, and that's good. They have expanded the restaurant menu, though, serving some genuine Florida Cracker cuisine—gator tail, turtle, frog (that's whole frog, not just the legs), as well as burgers and chili.

DIRECTIONS: Drive to the junction of SR 60, Highway 441, and the Florida Turnpike.

DON'T MISS: The Desert Inn

EGMONT KEY

Population: 0

BY THE TURN OF THE TWENTIETH CENTURY, 1.8-mile-long Egmont Key, just outside the entrance to Tampa Bay, had become home to over three hundred military personnel, who settled there following construction of Fort Dade at the onset of the Spanish-American War. Egmont Key became, in essence, a small town, with its own hospital, power plant, post office, movie theater, even a YMCA. The fort was deactivated in 1923, although Egmont served briefly during World War II as a military surveillance station. In 1939, the Coast Guard took over operation of Egmont Key's 87-foot-tall lighthouse. The island was designated a National Wildlife Refuge in 1974, and in 1989 Egmont Key became a state park. Today, Egmont Key's most

The beach at Egmont Key

recognizable structure is its lighthouse. The original lighthouse was built in 1848, but then was destroyed by a hurricane the same year. It was rebuilt in 1858. Although Fort Dade's brick streets remain, the buildings are gone. Some of the fortification bunkers remain, though they are partially submerged along the shore.

The Egmont Key Alliance is an active grassroots support organization dedicated to preserving Egmont Key's remaining historical structures and protecting the island's fragile ecological balance.

DIRECTIONS: Access by boat, or take the ferry from the Bay Pier at Fort DeSoto Park, St. Petersburg.

ANNA MARIA,
HOLMES BEACH

Population: Anna Maria 1,831; Holmes Beach 5,119

*T*HE TOWNS OF ANNA MARIA and Holmes Beach, on seven-and-a-half-mile-long Anna Maria Island, have been favorite convenient getaways for west coast Floridians since the early 1900s. In spite of its prime location south of the entrance to Tampa Bay and just offshore from Bradenton, Anna Maria Island has managed to fend off the usually inevitable invasion of high-rise condos and towering hotels to retain its easy-paced, beach-town flavor reminiscent of Florida's west coast beach towns in the 1950s and '60s.

Most people assume that the name Anna Maria has a Spanish origin, and that's a reasonable assumption, since Spanish explorers, including Ponce de León and Hernando de Soto, sailed this coast in the early 1500s. Old Spanish maps that predate Florida's inclusion in the United States label the island as Ana Maria Cay. Another contingent, however, claims that the name is Scottish and should be pronounced "Anna Mar-EYE-a." Many of the island's longtime residents pronounce the name with the long "i."

George Emerson Bean stopped on uninhabited Anna Maria Island sometime in the early 1890s while sailing from his home in Connecticut down to the Gulf. He fell in love with it and vowed to return with his family. In 1893, he filed for homestead on 160 acres on the north end of the island. With the help of his sons, he built the island's first residence near where the Rod & Reel Pier is now. Bean died in 1898, but his sons and their families continued to live and build on Anna Maria.

John Roser was the German baker who invented the recipe for Fig Newtons. He had sold his recipe to Nabisco and moved to St. Petersburg to retire when he met George Bean Jr. In 1911, they teamed up to form the Anna Maria Beach Company and began the first commercial development of the island. That same year, the city pier was built to serve as a dock for day-excursion boats from Tampa. It wasn't until 1921 that the Cortez Bridge opened, connecting Bradenton Beach at the south end of the island to the mainland. In 1913, John Roser built Anna Maria's first church as a memorial to his wife, Caroline. Each Saturday, a pastor from a different church on the mainland came to the nondenominational Roser Memorial Community Church by boat, gave Sunday services, and then returned on Monday. The church is at the northeast end of Pine Avenue and is still active today.

Anna Maria's main road, Gulf Drive, runs up the center of the island. For most of the Gulf side, in lieu of a beach road, a succession of two-block-long avenues with tree names like Palm, Willow, Cedar, Oak, and Maple dead-end at the beach. Pine Avenue–the exception– runs all the way east to the bay.

Good eateries abound on Anna Maria Island. Restaurateur Sean Murphy came to Holmes Beach in the mid-1980s (by way of New Orleans, where he worked at Arnaud's) to open Beach Bistro. It's right on the beach, but very upscale, with luscious entrées like cashew-and-coconut-crusted Floribbean Grouper and my favorite, Roasted Maple

Leaf Duck. On the north end of the island, The Sandbar has outdoor beachfront dining. The best places to grab a bite, however, are Anna Maria's much more casual beach dives, local diners that have a trail of beach sand leading through the front door. When I come to visit resident and long-time friend Andy Duncan, we alternate between two favorites: Duffy's and the Rod & Reel Pier.

Beer-and-burger joint Duffy's Tavern has been an Anna Maria icon since Duffy Whiteman opened it in 1958 in a screen-windowed shack on the north end of the island. Pat Guyer bought Duffy's in 1971. Although a popular locals' spot, there were also customers who would come from as far away as Tampa and Lakeland just for lunch. In 2003, Pat and her five daughters (who all work there) moved Duffy's to its current location on Gulf Drive. Same great atmosphere, cold beer, and great food, but now with air conditioning! I always get the same thing—a cheeseburger and a bowl of their killer chili. Pat Guyer, an Anna Maria icon herself, became very active in Anna Maria Island politics—she was on the city council for many years and was elected mayor of Holmes Beach in 1990. Sadly, in 2010, Pat Guyer passed away, and I think it is accurate to say the town lost its

Rod & Reel Pier and Café

Harrington House Bed & Breakfast

matriarch. The Guyer daughters (all with names that start with "P") continue the Duffy's tradition.

My other favorite Anna Maria beach diner is the Rod & Reel Pier and Café, around the north point of the island on the bay side. This 1947 two-story shack out on the end of the wooden pier has a bait-and-tackle shop downstairs and a tiny, short-order diner upstairs. Waves passing under the pier cause the wooden structure to sway gently back and forth. Looking northwest, diners have a view of Passage Key and Egmont Key and the Gulf beyond. To the northeast, they can see the Sunshine Skyway Bridge crossing the entrance to Tampa Bay. Good grouper sandwiches can be found at lots of Florida restaurants today, but for me the standard has been set by the grouper sandwich at the Rod & Reel Pier.

If all of this sounds enticing enough to keep you here for a weekend or maybe a week, accommodations range from a few small Mom-and-Pop motels to cottages and houses for rent. Then there is the Harrington House Bed & Breakfast on Holmes Beach. Oddly enough, Florida beachfront bed and breakfasts are somewhat rare. This three-story coquina-masonry, cypress-framed mansion was built in 1925 and opened as a bed and breakfast in 1989. Most of the second- and third-floor rooms have balconies with sweeping beach and Gulf views. With the addition of two adjacent properties, there are seventeen rooms, yet it still retains the comfortable, casual feel of a private beach home.

Great food, great beaches, great fishing, and a disdain for intrusive commercial development combine to make Anna Maria a perfect Florida beach town.

DIRECTIONS: Located west of Bradenton, take SR 64 to Holmes Beach. Turn north on Gulf Boulevard to Anna Maria.

DON'T MISS: Duffy's and the Rod & Reel Pier

CORTEZ

Population: 4,491

*C*ORTEZ MAY BE THE LAST of something once common-place in yesterday's Florida—a coastal commercial fishing town. It occupies the western tip of a point of land that juts out into Anna Maria Sound and can be reached from Bradenton Beach via Highway 684/Cortez Road Bridge. Almost everything in Cortez has some relationship to seafood, fishing, or boats. Signs along Cortez Road advertise smoked mullet, fresh shrimp, outboard motor repair, bait, and fishing charters.

On the south side of Highway 684/Cortez Road, you'll find a quiet neighborhood of simple clapboard cottages, many dating back to the 1920s. Boat docks and fish warehouses line the south shoreline.

In the mid-1800s, this peninsula was known as Hunter's Point. The locals called the area "the Kitchen" because of the abundance of seafood and shellfish caught in these waters. In 1888, a post office was established here, and the name Cortez was submitted. "Cortez" may be a reference to Spanish explorer Hernando Cortes, who conquered Mexico and the Aztecs for Spain in 1519. However, there is no indication that Cortes ever explored Florida.

The town grew into a small but busy fishing community, with mullet netting, processing, and shipping the primary industries. Much of Cortez's history is divided between "before 1921" and "after 1921," when a hurricane blew in from the Gulf without warning. A storm surge destroyed the docks and sank whole fleets of fishing boats. A large passenger steamship, the *Mistletoe,* went down in the storm. Residents crowded into the town's brick schoolhouse for shelter while their homes washed away. The only building left standing on Cortez's waterfront was the Albion Inn hotel.

At the south end of 23rd Street, on the south waterfront, you will find a two-story boatbuilder's shop, with living quarters upstairs nearly camouflaged by the palmetto scrubs, palm trees, and Australian pines that surround it. A sign over the front entranceway, hand-painted on well-weathered driftwood, reads "N. E. Taylor Boatworks." If you saw the 1998 movie *Great Expectations,* starring Gwyneth Paltrow and Ethan Hawke, you might recognize the building. 20th Century Fox used it as the setting for the main character's home in the modern adaptation of the Charles Dickens classic. N. E. Taylor Boatworks belongs to Alcee Taylor, who was born in Cortez in 1923, and grew up here. The upstairs was his family's home. The downstairs was his father's business, the Boatworks.

I got to spend some time with Alcee back in 1999, and he filled me in on his family history—along with some of Cortez's. "Sometime around nineteen oh eight, my father, Neriah Elijah Taylor, moved down from North Carolina. His brother had come first, and then he followed and brought my mother down," Alcee explained as we walked through the shop, which is now essentially a museum. "The foundation of this house and the siding was built from driftwood lumber that washed away from down at Longboat Pass during the storm of nineteen twenty-one. My father built boats in here."

Seventy-five years' worth of woodworking and boatbuilding equipment—every size and shape of saw, all variety of hand drills, jigs, and templates—fills what was once a small factory for building eighteen- to twenty-foot pole skiffs and twenty-two- to twenty-six-foot V-hull launches. Back then, two iron rails used for sliding completed boats down to the water ran the length of the floor, out the back door, and into the bay.

"In the middle there is where the cradle came up to pull boats out," Alcee explained as we carefully weaved our way around stacks of wood and materials used decades ago for constructing boats. He pointed out items of interest as we passed them. "There's one of the patterns used for building a skiff. And this here is a natural-crook cedar timber." He held up a hefty tree limb that had grown into an arc. "You had to go out into the mangrove swamps, off Longboat Key, to find pieces of wood with just the right bend in them to make your framing for the boat. They had to all line up, where you could carry the flare back on each side of the boat. You'd saw them down the center with the cross-cut saw and have two matching pieces, one for each side of the keel."

Alcee's two older brothers built boats with his father. Alcee didn't build them himself, but he did help haul lumber back from the woods. "There were a lot more mosquitoes back then," he recalled. "I've seen them so thick on the screen window upstairs that you had to beat the screen to get air to flow through."

In addition to displaying all of N. E. Taylor's boatbuilding equipment, Alcee has compiled a large collection of old photographs and newspaper articles. He showed me photos of the docks in Cortez before and after the 1921 hurricane. Then he pulled out a 1932 N. E. Taylor Boatworks invoice for a completed boat that read, "Boat: $350.00. Lumber: $65.00." They charged two dollars for a "pull-out" to winch the boat out of the water. He pulled out a receipt from Southern Utilities Company, dated June 12, 1925. "That's when we got electricity and lights put in the house."

The centerpiece of Alcee's museum is a 1936 donkey boat. Why is it called a donkey boat? "Back in them days they used tractors, Model-Ts, horses, mules, donkeys, whatever, to pull the nets in from the beaches. My dad had bought a motor that he was going to put

Docks in front of Star Fish Company Market

over there with the winch so he'd have power to pull up boats with. Some fishermen got to talking with him. They figured they could mount that motor in a boat, hook it to a truck transmission and a pulley, anchor the boat out in the water, run a rope out, and pull nets with it. That's what they did. It took the place of the donkey, so they called it a donkey boat."

When I asked Alcee about living his entire life in Cortez, he told me: "I do like Cortez. There are good folks here. You can still get out and walk around whenever and wherever you want to."

When I came through Cortez in 2009, I looked for Alcee again, but he was not in. At the Star Fish Company seafood market next door, I was assured that Alcee is still around and doing fine. If you happen to catch him in, he might give you a tour of his place. By the way, the Star Fish Market (in Cortez since 1923) has an open-air restaurant—dockside, behind the market—with fresh-off-the-boat seafood. Also, alongside the Cortez Bridge over to Bradenton Beach, you'll find Annie's Bait & Tackle, a great authentic old-Cortez dive bar and grill.

Annie's Bait and Tackle

Cortez has always appreciated the importance of its heritage and its connection to the sea. In 2007, the Florida Maritime Museum opened in Cortez's historic 1912 schoolhouse. The museum is a joint project undertaken by the Florida Institute of Saltwater Heritage, the Cortez Village Historical Society, and Manatee County. Exhibits include tools, equipment, and historic photographs from Cortez as well as from other historic fishing villages along Florida's Gulf coast.

Out on Cortez Road is another place that almost qualifies as a museum. At the warehouse-size Sea Hagg shop, you could spend days rummaging through the shelves of salvaged seagoing hardware—ship's wheels, portholes, propellers, and compasses, plus local artists' sculptures and paintings.

DIRECTIONS: From Bradenton Beach, cross the Highway 684 Bridge, or from I-75, take the Highway 70 exit, which leads to Highway 684/Cortez Road.

DON'T MISS: N. E. Taylor Boatworks

LAKE PLACID

Population: 1,985

*H*IGHWAY 27 RIDES ACROSS the Highlands County hills south of Sebring. From the road you can see for miles in any direction. Elevated vistas like these are not common in this region of Florida. But here, broad, rolling hills alternate with lakes in the low spots. Like a very small mountain range, the Lake Wales Ridge runs parallel to Highway 27 about twelve miles to the east. I think I know why Melvil Dewey fell in love with this area the first time he saw it.

In 1927, seventy-six-year-old Dr. Melvil Dewey—the same Dewey who invented the Dewey decimal library cataloging system—came to Florida in search of a southern version of his hometown, Lake Placid, New York. What Dewey envisioned was a resort that would mirror the Lake Placid Club, but with a milder climate in winter. He knew he had found what he was looking for when he first laid eyes on the small agricultural community of Lake Stearns. Dewey wasted no time in making arrangements with local landowners. In 1928, Lake Stearns incorporated under its new name, Lake Placid. Names of two of the surrounding lakes were also changed: Lake Childs became Lake Placid, and Lake Stearns became Lake June-in-Winter (The New York lake is simply Lake June.) Sadly, Dewey wasn't able to enjoy his newfound paradise for very long. Although Florida provided a welcome respite from his chronic bronchitis, Melvil Dewey passed away three years after moving here. But with plans already under way, his widow, Emily, continued to develop his dream. The Great Depression stunted progress in the early and mid-1930s, but ultimately Lake Placid grew into the attractive community that it is today. It is still growing, not so much in size but in character.

Looming over the horizon is the 270-foot-high Placid Tower. When it was built in 1960, it was the tallest concrete masonry structure in the world. Nearly five thousand tons of concrete and steel reinforcing went into its construction. The view from the open-air Eagle's Nest is spectacular, but unfortunately, the tower has been closed since 2007. The Chamber of Commerce reports that there have been potential buyers that would reopen it, but so far no deals have been struck.

Lake Placid's city limits extend only around the uptown area, which technically makes the city of Lake Placid only one and a quarter miles square. Lakes border it on two sides. Lake June-in-Winter wraps around the west side of uptown, with Lake Placid further to the south.

In August and September something special happens—east of town, thousands of acres of fields blossom with brightly colored caladium plants. Lake Placid is the Caladium Capital of the World. Ninety-five percent of those sold commercially around the world are grown right here in Highlands County. A temperate climate and an abundance of boggy muck-soil near the lakes make this area ideal for growing caladiums, though they're not native to Florida. Caladiums originated in the Amazon basin and were brought to the United States for the Chicago World's Fair in 1893. They were first grown commercially in Apopka in the 1920s. Occasional winter freezing temperatures forced

Cracker Trail Cattle Drive mural by artist Keith Goodson

the industry to move further south in the 1930s, eventually finding the perfect home in Lake Placid and Highlands County.

Just beyond the caladium fields is twenty-seven-thousand-acre Lake Istokpoga, famous worldwide for record-size largemouth bass. Avid bass fishermen from around the country make the pilgrimage here for tournaments or just a shot at landing a record lunker.

Ordinarily, I wouldn't put a grocery store on my list of things to see, but the Lake Placid Winn-Dixie on Highway 27 is different. On its outside south wall is a mural of epic proportions. At 35 feet high and 175 feet long, the mural is a panoramic depiction called *Cracker Trail Cattle Drive*. Artist Keith Goodson has painted a hauntingly realistic scene that shows Florida "Cracker" cowboys of yesteryear moving their herds across the southern plains of the state. The term "Cracker" comes from the cracking of the whips used to maneuver the herds of cattle, and it stuck as a nickname for Florida cowboys. Some of the cows almost seem to follow you from one end of the mural to the other. And if you listen closely, you'll hear the cracking whips and mooing cows of a Florida cattle drive. The Lake Placid Mural Society calls it "moosic"—it's piped through speakers on the roof to add another dimension to the mural experience.

Back in 1992 a group of local artists and art patrons came up with the idea of making Lake Placid a mural town. There are currently forty-four larger-than-life murals painted on walls throughout Lake Placid. Each portrays people, places, history, or wildlife of local significance. All (except for *Cracker Trail Cattle Drive*) are downtown. The best way to see them all is with the help of a guidebook available at the Lake Placid Mural Society's office.

Lake Placid's first mural, Tom Freeman's *Tea at Southwinds*, on the side of the Caladium Arts and Crafts Co-op building, was dedicated in May 1993. It depicts three elegantly dressed ladies enjoying an outdoor patio at the former Lakeside Inn in the 1940s. They represent the three ladies who founded the Caladium Arts and Crafts Co-op: Harriet Porter, Sue Ellen Robinson, and Carol Mills. The Co-op (at Interlake Boulevard and Pine Street) is a ten-thousand-square-foot store, gallery, and showcase for the work of its two hundred–plus members, all Highlands County artists and craftspeople.

Lake Placid has not only gained a reputation as an arts community and as the Caladium Capital, but also as the home of Toby's Clown School, where over a thousand graduates have gone on to become professional clowns.

DIRECTIONS: Drive sixteen miles south of Sebring on Highway 27.

DON'T MISS: The murals

ARCADIA

Population: 6,899

*V*ISITORS TO ARCADIA might note that a disproportion-
ate number of buildings downtown have "Built in 1906" noted on
them. On Thanksgiving night in 1905, downtown Arcadia suffered
a devastating fire. Apparently it began in a downtown livery stable,
but the cause was never determined. High winds rapidly spread the
flames. The townspeople fought valiantly to extinguish it, but at that
time Arcadia had no public water system or firefighting equipment.
By dawn, all but three buildings had been consumed. Miraculously,
no one died.

Two days later, Arcadia's business leaders passed the city's first
building codes, which stated that all reconstruction had to be done

with brick or concrete. Not long after, they built a city water supply and organized a fire department. Arcadia rose, like the proverbial phoenix from the ashes, to become a thriving south-central Florida community.

This is cattle country, and for more than eighty years, Arcadia has been nationally famous for its mid-March and July 4th All-Florida Championship Rodeos. In recent decades, Arcadia has also become popular for another kind of wrangling—for antiques. In four blocks along Oak Street (the town's main street), there are a dozen antique shops, plus the historic Heard Opera House Museum, which also contains an antique mall.

The Mediterranean-style Opera House, built in 1906, occupies an entire city block at the corner of Oak Street and Polk Avenue in the center of downtown. In the 1910s, Arcadians strolled up these steps on Saturday evenings to watch plays and traveling vaudeville shows. When silent movies emerged in the 1920s, this became the movie theater. Now the stage and dressing rooms have been converted into a museum. A 1902 Deere and Webbe (forerunner of the John Deere Company) horse buggy and an Indian dugout canoe of undetermined age—discovered at the bottom of the Peace River—dominate the stage. Props, costumes, handbills, and newspaper clippings from early Arcadia Opera House days hang on the walls. The signatures of performers along with the names of their performances are still visible where they were scrawled on the dressing room walls, as was the custom with traveling shows in the 1900s and 1910s. Old movie projectors, film reels, theater seats, and silent-movie equipment preserved from the 1920s and '30s are also on display.

Rodeos and antiques shopping aside, I really need only one reason to come to Arcadia: the vanilla peanut butter pie at Wheeler's Goody Café. Wheeler's began as Fiegel's Goody Café in 1929, when fifty cents would buy a good hot lunch. Alene Davis was a waitress at Fiegel's in the 1930s. She married the owner, C. B. Fiegel, and they ran the café together until he died in 1951. When Alene remarried, to Walter Wheeler, she changed the name to Wheeler's Goody Café. It changed hands again in 1994, 2002, and 2006. But even with different owners, the food remained the same—the best Southern home-cooked grub within a hundred miles, and the best homemade pies on the planet. Local owners of the Last Chapter Bookstore and Coffee House, Carl and Marie Wiley, are the current owners. The Wileys have done some remodeling—they added a side screen porch with more tables. In 2009, I made an incognito visit, just to make sure the new owners were upholding the tradition of great grub. I am pleased to report that my fried catfish, collard greens, and two slices of vanilla peanut butter pie were as delectable as always.

DIRECTIONS: Drive to the junction of Highway 17 and SR 70, twenty-five miles northeast of Port Charlotte.

DON'T MISS: Wheeler's Goody Café

SOUTHERN REGION

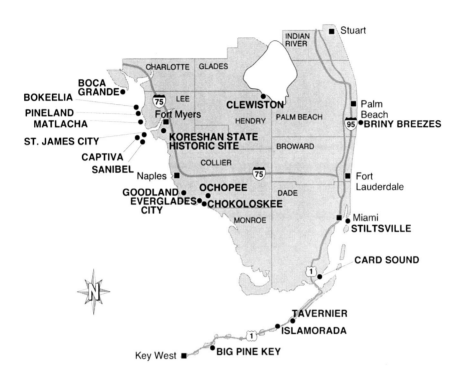

CHARLOTTE GLADES

INDIAN
RIVER

■ Stuart

BOCA
GRANDE ●

BOKEELIA

LEE

CLEWISTON

PINELAND

75 Fort Myers

PALM BEACH

■ Palm
Beach

MATLACHA

HENDRY

95 ●BRINY BREEZES

ST. JAMES CITY

KORESHAN STATE
HISTORIC SITE

BROWARD

CAPTIVA
SANIBEL

Naples ■

COLLIER

75

■ Fort
Lauderdale

GOODLAND ●
EVERGLADES●●CHOKOLOSKEE
CITY

OCHOPEE

DADE

● Miami
STILTSVILLE

MONROE

1

CARD SOUND

N

TAVERNIER

1 ● ISLAMORADA

Key West ■

●BIG PINE KEY

BOCA GRANDE

Population: 975

FOR THE BETTER PART OF A CENTURY, generations of Florida families have come to Boca Grande, on Gasparilla Island, for the relaxed island atmosphere, pristine beaches, and world-famous tarpon fishing.

For most of the 1800s, Gasparilla Island's few inhabitants were transient—some Cuban mullet fishermen and a few rumrunners. But in 1885, phosphate was discovered mid-state. Mining companies began transporting it by barge down the Peace River and out to Charlotte Harbor. Suddenly, Gasparilla Island, at the mouth of Charlotte Harbor, had become an important piece of property. The town of Boca Grande (Spanish for "big mouth," referring to Boca

Grande Pass at the mouth of Charlotte Harbor) sprung up at the island's southern end to accommodate workers unloading phosphate from river barges and reloading it onto ships sailing abroad. In 1907, the Charlotte Harbor and Northern Railroad line replaced the river barges.

The name Gasparilla Island conjures up the image of a debauched pirates' hideaway, and there is some history to back that up. Real pirates, like Henri Caesar and Brewster "Bru" Baker, did sail the southwestern coast of Florida and probably visited Gasparilla Island in the 1700s.

However, this area's most famous pirate, José Gaspar, was almost certainly a myth created out of tall tales told by an old Cuban fisherman, Juan "Panther Key John" Gomez, in the late 1800s. In 1918, the Charlotte Harbor and Northern Railroad released a publication, "The Gasparilla Story," which pieced together some of Gomez's anecdotes. It also contained sales advertisements for railroad-owned property in Boca Grande, the terminus of the railway on Gasparilla Island. Those early property sales efforts turned out to be lackluster, but the romanticized fable of José Gaspar became accepted as genuine. The truth is that Gasparilla Island was likely named after a Spanish priest who ran a mission in Charlotte Harbor. Old charts that predate Gaspar's presumed lifetime by two hundred years show Gasparilla Pass as Friar Gaspar Pass.

Today six-mile-long Gasparilla Island and the village of Boca Grande are still a kind of hideaway—accessible as they are only by a $4 toll bridge at its north end, or by boat or seaplane—but one that no longer attracts such notoriety. The relative isolation has allowed the area to develop a tranquil, tropical, laid-back personality. There are no stoplights, and the only structure more than three stories tall is a 1927 steel-girder lighthouse tower on the southern beach. Tin-roofed bungalows nestled among ghostly banyan trees make up the residential neighborhood, originally developed in the 1890s by (later Florida governor) Albert Gilchrist. The two oldest churches on the island are in this neighborhood. The United Methodist Church at Third Street and Gilchrist Avenue was built in 1910, and the First Baptist Church at Fourth Street and Gilchrist, in 1915. Back then, they would alternate Sunday services to ensure good attendance.

With a year-round population of less than a thousand, Boca Grande is uncrowded and unhurried. Residents get around in electric golf carts. There's even a golf cart path running the length of the northern half of the island, which leads into town.

"Downtown" Boca Grande contains an assortment of specialty shops, boutiques, galleries, and some outstanding restaurants. Its centerpiece is the restored 1911 Railroad Depot Building on Fourth Street at Park Avenue, where afternoon snackers line up for homemade ice cream at The Loose Caboose.

It is no surprise that fresh seafood is a specialty at Boca Grande restaurants. "Fresh catch" here really does mean that it was caught that morning. One of the best restaurants in town is Temptations, on Park Avenue. Temptations' interior is like a time capsule from 1947, the year it opened. It's the type of place where Humphrey Bogart might have hung out. Have whatever the "fresh catch" is with one of Temptations' outstanding sauces, like the Thai Sweet Chili. The tiny "Temp" Bar, next door, is *the* place to hear big-fish stories—just

Park Avenue

be mindful of the "Please No Profanity" sign behind the bar. Another longtime Boca Grande landmark restaurant, the Pink Elephant, is now operated by the Gasparilla Inn (across the street). Seared Crab cakes, Chargrilled Lamb Chops, and Almond-crusted Cedar Plank Salmon are just a few of the excellent entrées offered there. The Pink Elephant's desserts are deservedly famous—particularly the restaurant's Key Lime Pie, which is as rich and dense as a New York cheesecake. More casual eateries include: PJ's Seagrille on Park Avenue, Eagle Grille at the Boca Grande Marina, and the aforementioned Loose Caboose in the historic train depot.

Besides fishing and walking the shell-strewn beaches, visitors to Boca Grande pass the time browsing the shops, including Fugate's, Boca Grande's beach supplies, gifts, and sundries store at 4th Street and Park Avenue, opened in 1916. It is the oldest continuously operated business on the island and is still run by the Fugate family. It reminds me of the beach sundry shops that I recall from summer visits to Indian Rocks Beach in the 1960s. At Boca Grande Outfitters, a block south of Fugates, you'll find the best selection of fishing gear, sportswear, and outdoor clothing.

Boca Grande has some wildlife too. The island is home to a variety of seabirds—pelicans, herons, and egrets—and there are plenty of raccoons. Also, a few decades back, someone let a pair of pet iguanas loose. Now, their many descendents are frequently spotted sunning on the seawalls.

South of town you will find Boca Grande's two lighthouses. One, a 105-foot-tall, steel-girder structure built in 1927, stands alongside the public beach on Gulf Boulevard. The other, at the southern tip of the island, serves as a channel marker for Boca Grande Pass. Built in 1890, it is thought to be the oldest building on Gasparilla Island. It fell into disrepair in the 1960s, but was restored, and then recommissioned in 1986. The Boca Grande Lighthouse Museum opened there in 1999.

For another look at Boca Grande history, visit Whidden's Marina, bayside on 1st Street. This two-story tin-roof marina was listed on the National Register of Historic Places in 2000, and remains virtually unchanged since Sam Whidden built it in 1926. It is a functioning museum, as it is still operating as a marina and still being run by the Whidden family, who dedicated one section of the building to a

1927 Boca Grande Lighthouse

maritime museum that chronicles the history of Boca Grande from the 1920s to the present.

Most visitors to Boca Grande rent or own vacation homes, but there are two notable lodgings for tourists within walking distance of downtown. The first is the historic Gasparilla Inn, originally known as the Hotel Boca Grande when the palatial hotel was built in 1911. In 1930, industrialist and developer Barron G. Collier bought it and added a solarium and columns to the front entrance. Today, it is an opulent resort in the tradition of Collier's era, with a golf course, tennis courts, swimming pools, and a full-service spa. The main hotel has 154 rooms. Nineteen additional quadruplex cottages (which can be opened up to accommodate families or groups) occupy several blocks in the surrounding neighborhood. Citrus trees, Australian pines, and towering palms grow throughout the grounds. Around the corner on Fourth Street, The Anchor Inn offers just four rooms—two suites and two studios, all with kitchenettes—in a house built in 1925.

For decades treasure hunters have sifted the sands of Gasparilla Island and the other barrier islands around it in search of buried

Gasparilla Inn

pirate treasure. Very little of value has been found. But as it turns out, the sand itself is worth its weight in gold; the mythical pirate's island and its village of Boca Grande are the real treasure.

DIRECTIONS: From I-75, take exit #179 (North Port/ Toledo Blade Road), go east on Toledo Blade Road, cross Highway 41, continue east to Highway 776 and turn right, follow 776 to 771 (Gasparilla Road) and turn left, and then follow 771 to Boca Grande Causeway and turn left again.

DON'T MISS: The Temptation Restaurant and Fugate's

CLEWISTON

Population: 7,107

*C*LEWISTON, ON THE SOUTH BANK of Lake Okeechobee, is the capital of Florida's sugarcane country. United States Sugar Corporation, the country's largest and oldest sugarcane producer, has had its headquarters in Clewiston since the 1920s, when it was the Southern Sugar Company. U.S. Sugar farms on 175,000 acres in three counties that border Lake Okeechobee's south side.

The noble Clewiston Inn, the oldest hotel on Lake Okeechobee, is in the center of town at the corner of Sugarland Highway (Highway 27) and Royal Palm Avenue. Originally built in 1926, the inn was destroyed by a fire in 1937. U.S. Sugar rebuilt the inn in 1938 to accommodate and entertain visiting executives and dignitaries.

Four two-story columns support a traditional Southern gable that protrudes over the inn's entrance. Neatly pruned palm trees line the circular drive where it swings underneath the gable. This is a Rhett-and-Scarlett kind of place. Bird's-eye cypress paneling covers the lobby walls all the way up to its open-beam ceiling. The terra cotta tile floor is waxed to a glossy shine. A wide staircase with brass railings leads to the second floor. The rooms are comfortable and decorated in a simple yet elegant 1940s style. When you check in, you'll receive a bag of sugar cookies. This is, after all, the "Sweetest Town in America."

I came to the inn because I had heard about the J. Clinton Shepherd oil-on-canvas mural that wraps around all four walls in the inn's Everglades Lounge. Shepherd lived at the inn for the better part of 1945. Every day he took treks into the Everglades to sketch Florida's native wild animals and plants. When he felt that he had accumulated enough material, he began to put his subjects on canvas. The result is a hauntingly beautiful and remarkably real 360-degree panorama, set in an early morning mist and depicting most of the wildlife that calls the Everglades home. Every variety of native duck, egret, heron, and crane can be found somewhere on these walls. Owls, jays, and ospreys also make an appearance, as do deer, opossums, a marsh hare, raccoons, alligators, and a black bear with her cub. The mural is one continuous scene. Shepherd had to precisely measure and cut the canvas to fit around windows, cabinets, and the doorway. You almost feel as though you're standing in the middle of a cypress bay head at daybreak.

The inn has been at the center of life in Clewiston throughout the town's history. During World War II, the British Royal Air Force trained cadets at nearby Riddle Field. The Clewiston Inn was the flyboys' favorite hangout. The inn's caretakers have done an excellent job of adhering to the ambiance of that grand era.

This area's biggest attraction is what the Seminole Indians called the "Big Water." More than 730 square miles in area and 35 miles in diameter, Lake Okeechobee is a virtual inland sea. It is the second largest freshwater lake wholly within the United States' boundaries. To avid anglers, it is paradise. They come here for largemouth bass, bluegill, speckled perch, and Okeechobee catfish.

On September 16, 1928, tragedy struck Lake Okeechobee when a hurricane with 160-mile-per-hour winds crossed the lake from the Atlantic Ocean. The hurricane's front winds pushed the water in Lake Okeechobee to the north, flooding the town of Okeechobee. As it passed over, moving west, the winds from the backside of the hurricane pushed the water back south and flooded Pahokee, Belle Glade, and Clewiston. The Clewiston Inn survived, but more than two thousand people around Lake Okeechobee drowned. Rescuers continued to find bodies weeks after the storm. Many of them were Bahamian migrant workers, and there was no way to identify them. In response to that disaster, in the early 1930s, the U. S. Army Corps of Engineers built 140 miles of forty-foot-high levees around the lake, which you will see if you are driving east out of Clewiston.

DIRECTIONS: Take Highway 27 to the southwest side of Lake Okeechobee.

DON'T MISS: J. Clinton Shepherd's wildlife mural in the Clewiston Inn's Everglades Lounge

BRINY BREEZES

Population: 405

*B*RINY BREEZES–The Little Trailer Park That Could. The reason it could is that it sits on prime beach property, twenty minutes south of posh Palm Beach.

By the 1920s, the price of a Ford Model T had dropped to under $300 (down from $850 when it was introduced in 1909). That changed vacationing forever. Roads were being paved to all corners and now everyday folks could take automobile trips–and they did, in droves. Those early "tin-can tourists" lived and camped out of their automobiles, and campgrounds sprung up to accommodate them. Back in the 1930s Briny Breezes was a strawberry pasture, until farmer Ward Miller figured out that he could make more money parking cars and trailers on it than picking strawberries. In the 1950s he began selling lots outright to regulars, and by 1963 the property was owned entirely by residents, who decided to incorporate as the town of Briny Breezes. In 2005 a developer offered to buy all forty-two acres of Briny Breezes for what amounted to about $1 million per trailer lot. It stirred quite a debate among the mostly retiree residents, but in 2007 the deal fell through.

DIRECTIONS: Travel on Florida Highway A1A one mile south of Boynton Beach.

MATLACHA, BOKEELIA, PINELAND, ST. JAMES CITY

Population: Matlacha 735; Bokeelia 1,997; Pineland 444; St. James City 4,105

STATE ROAD 78 is the only bridge that connects mainland Fort Myers to Pine Island. But before reaching the island, you will pass through the curious little mile-long village of Matlacha (pronounced "Mat-la-*shay*"), a place so splashed in bright colors it's as if a Sherwin-Williams truck had a head-on collision with a DuPont truck. Matlacha resides on the tiny stepping-stone islands along the bridge to Pine Island. Fishing boats bob up and down at their moorings behind restaurants, gift shops, and galleries that line both sides of the highway. For many decades prior to the completion of the bridge in 1927, local fishermen had worked these exceptionally fertile fishing

177

Bert's Bar & Grill

grounds in the pass. When the bridge was built, some of them put up squatters' shacks alongside it. Before long, it evolved into the village of Matlacha. Fishing is still big here. They even call the SR 78 bridge the "Fishingest bridge in the world."

Matlacha has become an artists' enclave as well. Many of Leoma Lovegrove's vivid, large-scale acrylic paintings depict Florida wildlife, but she has a thing for musicians too—particularly the Beatles. Her Lovegrove Gallery is filled with spectacular original art and is a must-see. Next door, Wild Child Gallery features work from many local artists who work in a variety of mediums: painting, sculpture, photography, and jewelry design. Across the street at tiny Elena's, the owner has been creating her unique style of island jewelry for twenty years. These are just a few of dozens of galleries and artists' studios. There is good food here too. Bert's Bar & Grille has been a fixture since the 1930s. In the '40s, '50s, and '60s it was also a motel with a somewhat nefarious reputation. Today it's a great spot for live music and a grouper sandwich. For breakfast the Perfect Cup packs them in—I can vouch for their blueberry pancakes.

On my last visit I stayed at Matlacha Island Cottages, made

Matlacha Island Cottages

up of four nicely renovated historic waterfront cottages that match perfectly with the island's ambience. Each has a kitchenette, as well as its own backyard picnic area and private dock. Another option is the Bridgewater Inn, an eight-room motel, built on pylons over the water. You can fish right from the front door of your room.

Continue over the bridge and you will end up on seventeen-mile-long, three-mile-wide Pine Island—Florida's largest Gulf Coast island. SR 78 intersects Stringfellow Road, the island's main thoroughfare, which connects St. James City at its southern tip with Bokeelia at its northern tip. The straight, two-lane Stringfellow passes tropical groves and nurseries. Pine Island has a thriving subtropical exotic fruit and plant industry. Best known for its mangoes, which early settlers began growing here at the turn of the century, the island also supports pineapple, carambola, papaya, loquat, and palm trees.

Bokeelia, at the north end, is a popular launching point for fishing expeditions. The waters that surround Pine Island regularly yield snook, cobia, snapper, and redfish, in addition to the granddaddy of them all—tarpon.

Bokeelia's Main Street dead-ends at Capt'n Con's Fish House. This was Bokeelia's first house, built by H. W. Martin in 1904. Martin's wife ran the place as a boardinghouse for boat passengers and fishermen. Now the two-story, wood-frame structure is a popular seafood restaurant. The smaller house on its west side was Bokeelia's first post office.

The Crossed Palms Gallery, a block east of Capt'n Con's, is an art lover's wonderland. They have an eclectic collection of paintings, sculpture, pottery, pop art, and batiks. Owner Nancy Brooks has a knack for discovering exceptionally talented artists as yet unknown in the art world. The gallery's collection varies widely from serious to whimsical. There are grand, almost mural-size watercolors in one room and comical, brightly colored ceramic or papier-mâché animal sculptures in the next. Of particular note are the large scenic-Florida watercolors by Crossed Palms mainstay David Belling.

A few miles south of Bokeelia, wind down Pineland Road to Waterfront Drive in Pineland and you will come across the restored 1926 Tarpon Lodge and Restaurant, a gracious retreat tucked away on the west side of the island. There are twenty-one rooms in the main lodge and an adjacent stilt house, plus additional accommodations in a cottage and a boathouse.

In St. James City, at the southern end of Pine Island, I have found another great small-town eatery—the Waterfront Restaurant, housed in St. James City's first schoolhouse. The school building was erected in 1887. It survived a fire in 1896 and was moved twice before being settled into its current location. In the late 1940s, it became a fish camp. The wood-paneled interior has a rustic, old-Florida feel. The bar, which is in the classroom of the original school, has a canoe

Crossed Palms Gallery

hanging from the ceiling with hundreds of dollar bills taped to its hull. Once again, I recommend the grouper sandwich, but you won't miss with anything on the menu.

Pine Island has its own museum: Museum of the Islands, opened in 1990, just north of the intersection of Stringfellow Road and SR 78. History buffs will want to spend some time here to learn about this region's past. For instance, some famous figures in early Florida history stopped at Pine Island. According to his logs, Ponce de León careened his ship along the western shore in 1513. He and his crew spent several days repairing the ship's hull, gathering wood, and collecting fresh water. He returned to Pine Island in 1521 and, during a skirmish here with the Calusa Indians, was shot with an arrow. His crew took him to Cuba to recuperate, but he died there as a result of his wound.

Much of Pine Island's history predates written record. The Calusa lived on Pine Island for more than a thousand years before Ponce de León came. They built huge shell mounds and dug elaborate canals across the island. The arrival of the Spanish ultimately brought on the

Waterfront Restaurant

Calusa tribe's demise. They had no immunity to European diseases, most notably chickenpox. By the mid-1700s, they were all gone. Although the rumors are largely unsubstantiated, Pine Island Sound may have also been a haven for pirates—including Brewster "Bru" Baker, who may have lived for a while near present-day Bokeelia, and Henri "Black" Caesar, reported to have camped on nearby Sanibel Island.

DIRECTIONS: From I-75, take the North Fort Myers/SR 78 exit (Exit 143). Take SR 78 west.

DON'T MISS: Gallery browsing in Matlacha and The Crossed Palms Gallery in Bokeelia

SANIBEL, CAPTIVA

Population: Sanibel 5,577; Captiva 379

*S*ANIBEL AND CAPTIVA are two Gulf Coast barrier islands almost always mentioned in the same breath. They're next to
each other, and you must drive through Sanibel to get to Captiva.
However, they have distinctly different personalities.

Sanibel is famous for its gorgeous, shell-strewn beaches and its
casual (but still ritzy) boutiques, but there are natural and historic
sights here as well.

At the island's eastern tip, the one-hundred-foot-tall iron-frame
Sanibel Lighthouse has guided ships since its completion in 1884,
but it was almost lost before it ever went up. The lighthouse had
been built in sections and brought down by ship from New Jersey.

Sanibel lighthouse

Just a few miles offshore from Sanibel, the ship ran aground and sank. Salvagers, or "wreckers," mostly from Key West, were able to retrieve the sections from the bottom, and construction went forward as planned. It has been a National Landmark since 1972 and is still functional. At the Sanibel Historical Village and Museum, located on Dunlop Road near the intersection of Periwinkle Way and Tarpon Bay Road, you can see a collection of restored 1910s–1930s Sanibel frame houses and buildings.

Local Sanibel shell-collecting club members started a museum project that took ten years to realize. Finally, in 1995, on property donated by the Sanibel-pioneer Bailey family, the Bailey-Matthews Shell Museum opened its doors. The museum contains extensive exhibits on shellfish and has also become a renowned scientific and education resource.

Sanibel's paramount natural attraction is the J. N. "Ding" Darling National Wildlife Refuge, which occupies six thousand acres on the island's north end. Visitors can drive or hike through the refuge and see a wide variety of Florida wildlife, including alligators, turtles, otters, and raccoons. Bird watchers are in heaven here. Several hundred bird species make the refuge their home, among them pink-winged roseate spoonbills, blue herons, white ibis, egrets, owls, and ospreys. The refuge is named after political cartoonist Jay Norwood "Ding" Darling. Darling won a Pulitzer Prize in 1924 and 1943 and later was head of the U.S. Biological Survey and founder of the National Wildlife Foundation. Darling spent his winters on Sanibel and Captiva and championed the cause of conservation and wildlife preservation here, long before it was fashionable. As far back as the 1920s, Darling's cartoons reflected his concerns about conservation. It was his efforts that led to Sanibel and Captiva being declared wildlife sanctuaries by the State of Florida in 1948.

Remote Florida tropical islands where you can truly "get away from it all" but still arrive by car are a rare commodity; Captiva Island is a hardy holdout. To get any more remote you would need a boat or a seaplane, or would need to be an exceptionally good swimmer. Once you cross the short bridge that spans Blind Pass, which separates the two islands, there is a noticeable shift in topography. Captiva is more wildly vegetated, more rustic, and less populated. It is almost Polynesian in its tropical-ness. Dense flora–sea grapes, frangipani, crotons, spiny aloe, and all varieties of palm, including sable, coconut, royal, butterfly, and cabbage–inhabit the island.

One-block-long Andy Rosse Lane qualifies as Captiva's "downtown," with the circa-1920s Captiva Island Store (originally a schoolhouse) at one end and the Mucky Duck–a British-style pub and

Island Store

restaurant on the beach—at the other end. In between there are a few funky art galleries and shops. I like the Jungle Drums Gallery, which features original wildlife-theme art, sculpture, and furniture, much of it created by the gallery's owners, Jim and Kathleen Mazzotta.

There are terrific restaurants on both islands. The aforementioned Mucky Duck has a varied menu ranging from burgers to a very tasty duck a l'orange. One of my perennial favorite Captiva restaurants, the Sunshine Seafood Café, was purchased by Fort Myers restaurateur Sandra Stilwell in 2003. She remodeled, doubling the seating space, but kept chef Tao Diaz and his Pan-Asian/Floribbean/Italian menu of outstanding wood-grilled entrées. A kid's favorite eatery is the Bubble Room—a cross between a theme park and a restaurant, and known for its towering desserts. Just over the Sanibel side of the Blind Pass Bridge and right on the beach, the Mad Hatter Restaurant has a delectable menu of mouth-watering entrées like maple-syrup-glazed grouper and walnut-and-cherry-pesto-crusted rack of lamb. Sanibel Bean, on the north end of Sanibel and close to Captiva, is the locals' coffee, bakery, and breakfast meet-up spot, with dog-friendly outdoor

Mucky Duck Restaurant

seating. Two more Sanibel eateries that I like are Doc Ford's Sanibel Rum Bar & Grill (named for local novelist Randy Wayne White's series protagonist) and the Twilight Café with its mix of Thai-influenced and Italian dishes.

Although there is plenty of upscale lodging on both islands (like the South Seas Island Resort at Captiva's north end) my two favorites are low-key and beach casual. The Castaways sits just across Blind Pass on the Sanibel side. Nothing fancy, just simple 1940s- and '50s-era, wood-frame beach cottages and duplex cottages with screened porches and worn wood floors. Ten of the thirty units are right on the beach.

The 'Tween Waters Inn is across the bridge, near Captiva Island's narrowest point between the Gulf and Pine Island Sound. The inn has a long history here. Captiva's first settlers arrived in the late 1800s and early 1900s, long after the pirates who frequented these waters had been vanquished. One settler was Dr. J. Dickey from Bristol, Virginia. Dickey visited Captiva on a fishing trip in 1900, and then returned with his family in 1905. Since there were no schools on Captiva, Dickey also brought along a tutor, Miss Reba Fitzpatrick, to educate his children. He built a schoolhouse with living quarters for Miss Reba upstairs. Mr. and Mrs. Bowman Price, friends of the Dickeys' from Bristol, purchased the schoolhouse and surrounding property in 1925. In 1931, they converted the old school into the 'Tween Waters Inn. Over the years, the Prices added cottages to accommodate new visitors who arrived every winter. In the late 1940s, they floated army barracks across the sound from Fort Myers to add more cottages.

Some famous people made the 'Tween Waters their winter retreat. Anne Morrow Lindbergh, prolific author and wife of Charles Lindbergh, stayed here in the 1950s. She wrote one of her best known works, *Gift from the Sea,* while on Captiva. Cartoonist "Ding" Darling (see reference above) frequented the 'Tween Waters too. He would rent two cottages: #103 as his room and #105 as his studio.

Do a little back roads exploring and you'll eventually run across another quaint piece of Captiva history—the Chapel by the Sea. Captiva's earliest settler, William Binder, built the tiny white chapel on Chapin Road in 1901 as a schoolhouse. Binder was shipwrecked off Captiva in 1885 and was the first to file a homestead claim on the island. Next to the chapel, the Captiva Cemetery is shaded by gumbo-limbo trees. The high spot shared by the chapel and cemetery is an ancient Calusa Indian shell midden.

Directions to Sanibel and Captiva islands:
From I-75, take Fort Myers Exit #131 (Daniels Parkway). Travel west to Summerlin Road, turn left, follow Summerlin approximately 10 miles, and then cross the Sanibel Causeway to Sanibel Island. To get to Captiva, head north on Periwinkle Way until it ends, then turn right on Tarpon Road, and then left on Sanibel-Captiva Road, and drive 7 miles across the Blind Pass Bridge on to Captiva.

DON'T MISS: The J. N. "Ding" Darling National Wildlife Refuge

KORESHAN STATE
HISTORIC SITE

Population: 0

THE KORESHAN STATE HISTORIC SITE, along the shore of the Estero River, is the setting for one of the oddest chapters in Florida history. In 1869, Dr. Cyrus Teed, a medical doctor living near Syracuse, New York, experienced what he labeled "an illumination, a vision." Teed had recently become disgruntled with conventional medicine and had begun studying metaphysics. During this illumination, according to Teed, a list of universal truths was revealed to him by an angel. Following that experience, he felt compelled to form an organization based on what he had divined. His initial attempts in New York failed, but in 1886 in Chicago, he generated enough of a following to incorporate his so-called College of Life. Two years later, he opened a communal home there where his followers could reside. Cyrus Teed adopted the name Koresh (which is ancient Hebrew for Cyrus). His organization evolved into the Koreshan Unity, and his doctrine became known as Koreshanity. In 1894, Teed purchased three hundred acres in Florida along the Estero River from German immigrant Gustave Damkohler (one of the earliest settlers in what is now Estero) on which to begin building a communal "New Jerusalem." Dr. Teed envisioned an enormous, hub-shaped city, large enough to be home to ten million people. His detailed plan included such far-thinking ideas as underground passageways to carry out refuse, which would then be recycled and returned as compost.

Of course, the plan never came to fruition. People who visit here regularly comment, "Is it any wonder that they died out? They didn't believe in reproducing!" This is a common misunderstanding. It's true that Dr. Teed and the Koreshans believed in a celibate lifestyle, but only for those who worked full-time in the leadership, governing, and operation of the commune. These people lived in separate dormitories, while Koreshans who had families lived in outlying cottages. Teed counted on outside recruits to grow their numbers.

Teed's beliefs had some vague basis in Christianity, although he believed that the Bible was written symbolically and required the interpretation of a prophet. Koreshanity mixed theological, sociological, and (supposed) scientific theories into one philosophy. One of his most bizarre beliefs was something called "Cellular Cosmogony," which purported that the surface of the Earth was on the inside lining of a giant sphere, and that the sun (which revolved and had both a light and a dark side), the planets, and space existed in the center of that sphere. Teed was so intent on convincing the scientific community that this was indeed the case that he staged an experiment to prove it. The Koreshan Unity's "geodetic" staff constructed an enormous accordion-like contraption, which they named the "Rectilineater," to prove their hypothesis. It stretched out from the beach into Estero Bay. No one really seems to understand exactly what it was supposed to measure, but the geodetic staff claimed that it substantiated their theory. They were so confident in their findings that they offered $10,000 to anyone who could disprove them. Apparently no one ever bothered to challenge them.

Granted, there were some peculiarities about these folks, but unlike most other religious cults and communes, the Koreshans were inclusive. They interacted happily with and were a part of the surrounding communities. They always welcomed outsiders and never condemned others for disagreeing with their doctrine. They were also very industrious people. They farmed citrus, shipped fruit, operated printing presses, and ran a sawmill, a boat-building business, a general store, a bakery, and eventually a restaurant. They even had their own concert band, which was quite popular at the time. The Koreshan Unity continued to acquire property, and in 1904 owned about seventy-five hundred acres.

Cyrus "Koresh" Teed died in 1908, and the Koreshan Unity's population began a slow decline. In 1961, the handful of remaining Koreshans donated the Koreshan Unity property to the State of Florida to become a state historic site. Hedwig Michel was the last president of the Koreshan Unity and the last living Koreshan. She died in 1982 at age ninety.

The Koreshans and their beliefs may have died out, but the remains of their odd world and existence have been well preserved at the Koreshan State Historic Site.

DIRECTIONS: From I-75, take the CR 850/Corkscrew Road exit (Exit 123) west 2 miles.

GOODLAND

Population: 300

FROM THE TOP OF THE STATE ROAD 92 bridge over Goodland Bay at the western edge of the Ten Thousand Islands, you get a brief glimpse of Marco Island's high-rise beach condos on the horizon, five miles away. But turn left immediately after the bridge and you'll find a completely different ambience in the tiny fishing community of Goodland. A few homesteaders settled here at "Goodland Point" back in the late 1800s, but more people started coming eighty years ago after the first Goodland bridge, an old wooden swing bridge, was built in 1935. In contrast to the beach side of Marco Island, Goodland hasn't grown much since then, and that's the way folks here like it. What it lacks in size, it makes up for in personality.

Today, as then, fishing is the main draw, and to keep those visitors

Stan's Idle Hour restaurant and bar

(and the few locals) watered and fed, there are three bar-and-grills, all with good local fresh seafood. The first one you come to is Stan's Idle Hour Seafood Restaurant. Owner Stan Gober is Goodland's Renaissance man–restaurateur, singer/song-writer, stand-up comic, and festival promoter. Stan's Idle Hour has been hosting Goodland's Annual Mullet festival (in January, always the weekend prior to Super Bowl) since the 1980s, which culminates in the crowning of that year's "Buzzard Lope Queen," named for a Stan Gober song and locals' favorite dance.

Next door at the Little Bar Restaurant, the sign says "New Little Bar and Restaurant," but most of the decorations and accoutrements inside are relics salvaged from old bars around the country, which makes the place interesting to browse through. Around the corner is the Old Marco Lodge Crab House in an 1869 house once owned by the Collier Family, and moved here from the other side of the island in 1964.

DIRECTIONS: Take State Road 92 south from Highway 41/ Tamiami Trail, cross the bridge, and turn left immediately.

DON'T MISS: Stan's Idle Hour restaurant and bar

EVERGLADES CITY, CHOKOLOSKEE, AND OCHOPEE

Population: Everglades City 616; Chokoloskee 404; Ochopee 128

*F*LORIDA'S NETHERWORLD EVERGLADES is the largest subtropical wilderness in the United States, occupying much of the southern end of the peninsula. Technically it is an immensely broad river, in some places more than half the width of the state. The "river" trickles south, primarily out of Lake Okeechobee. With only a fifteen-foot drop in elevation from Okeechobee to Florida Bay, the flow is nearly imperceptible. Although most of the Everglades sits underwater, it is seldom more than a foot deep. Water evaporating from the Everglades supplies most of the southern portion of the state's rainfall. Scientists call it the hydrologic cycle—a perpetual rain-generating machine. At one time this Everglades system was considerably larger than it is now, but canals have drained and diverted much of the water from its northern and central sections to the state's heavily populated southeast coast.

Everglades National Park actually encompasses only the lower fifth—about 1.4 million acres—of the entire Everglades. The lower east-west stretch of US Highway 41/Tamiami Trail marks the park's northern boundary. Another 720,000 acres on the north side of US Highway 41/Tamiami Trail was designated the Big Cypress National Preserve in 1974. In 1989, President Bush signed into law the Everglades National Park Protection and Expansion Act, enlarging Everglades National Park by an additional 107,000 acres on its east side.

From the Tamiami Trail, the Everglades appears to be just an endless expanse of saw grass, slash pine bay heads, and swamp. Closer observation reveals that it's brimming with wildlife. Over three hundred species of birds call the Everglades home; among them are ospreys, bald eagles, blue herons, great egrets, wood ibis, anhingas, pink roseate spoonbills, and purple gallinules. One of the rarest—the Everglades snail kite—lives here too and feeds exclusively on apple snails.

There is far less chance that you'll see a Florida panther, our state mammal, although this is its natural habitat. Park rangers estimate that there are less than a hundred of these beautiful animals left in the wild. It's also unlikely that you'll see any of the few crocodiles that live in a remote southeast section of the park. Everglades National Park is the only place in the United States where they coexist with their broader-snouted relatives, alligators. In contrast, alligators can be found throughout the state, and in vast numbers in the Everglades. Placed on the Endangered Species List in the late 1960s, these prehistoric reptiles made an astounding comeback and were removed from the list in 1987.

Turn-of-the-twentieth-century federal and state leaders saw the Everglades as a colossal nuisance—a swamp that needed to be drained. This was a popular enough opinion in 1904 that Governor Napoleon Broward was elected on a platform of promising to do just that. Dredging and canal-building efforts to drain the Everglades began in 1906 and continued in earnest into the late 1920s, during which time a series of canals were built to redirect water from Lake Okeechobee over to developing cities on the Atlantic "Gold" coast. The old adage about buying or selling swamp land in Florida has its origins here. Governor Broward generated much publicity with his plans to reclaim the Everglades, and plots of "swamp land" began to sell like hotcakes. Of course, as it turned out, these properties were worthless to the hapless buyers. Then, in 1928, one of the most devastating hurricanes in Florida history cut across Lake Okeechobee, flooding the towns on its perimeter and killing more than 1,800 people. Congress' answer to that tragedy was the River and Harbor Act of 1930, which authorized the U.S. Army Corps of Engineers to build forty-foot-high levees around the entire southern shoreline and portions of the northern shoreline of Lake Okeechobee in an effort to contain future hurricane flooding. What they didn't understand was that in doing so, they were constricting the heart that pumped water through the Everglades. In what seems now like a contradiction, only four years later Congress authorized the Everglades National Park Project. It would take thirteen additional years before the park was actually created.

By the 1940s some began to recognize the vital role the Everglades played in the climatological and ecological balance of the state. Perhaps the most valiant of them was *Miami Herald* columnist and author Marjory Stoneman Douglas. Her book *The Everglades: River of Grass* was published in 1947, the same year Everglades National Park finally opened. For the next fifty years she fought vigorously against human encroachment on the Everglades. In the 1960s, while in her late seventies, she became involved with the Audubon Society of Miami's efforts to halt the building of an international airport in the Everglades. Society members pleaded with her to start an organization that would unite the efforts of those concerned with the fate the Everglades. She did, and Friends of the Everglades is an organization that is still today one of the most powerful voices for the area's preservation. Proving that good people do not always die young, Marjory Stoneman Douglas passed away in 1998 at the age of 108.

Prior to 1923, Everglades City, southeast of Naples, had been a sleepy fishing village and trading outpost. Barron Collier put it on the map when he made it the Collier County seat, as well as his company town, from which construction operations of the Tampa-to-Miami "Tamiami" Trail took place. Construction on the "Trail" had first begun in 1915, but by 1922 the State of Florida had run out of funds needed to complete the last section from Naples to Miami, across the Everglades. Barron Collier, originally from Tennessee, had made millions with his New York City Consolidated Street Railway Advertising Company. He reinvested his earnings in real estate and development, and by the early 1920s had accumulated over a million acres in southwest Florida, making him the largest single land owner in the state at that time. The Tamiami Trail was crucial to the appreciation of Colliers' real estate holdings, so he proposed an idea to the state: If they would divide Lee County and create a new southern county, he would finance and oversee the completion of the Trail through the Everglades. They agreed (and named the county "Collier"). It took five years of digging, dredging, and dynamiting, but on April 26, 1928, the Tamiami Trail officially opened.

After Hurricane Donna thrashed Everglades City in 1960, Collier pulled the last of his interests out of the town. The county seat moved to Naples, and Everglades City settled back into the quiet fishing village that it once was, and still is today.

Everglades City's Rod and Gun Club—a three-story, clapboard lodge, overlooks the Barron River. The city's original founder, W. S. Allen, built it in 1850. Its second owner, George W. Storter, enlarged it to accommodate hunters, sport fishermen, and yachting parties that were coming to the Everglades in increasing numbers each winter season. Barron Collier bought it in 1922 and operated it as a private club for his fellow industrial magnates and political dignitaries. Through the years such luminaries as Herbert Hoover, Franklin D. Roosevelt, Dwight and Mamie Eisenhower, and Richard Nixon have all been guests at the Rod and Gun Club.

Today the Rod and Gun Club is still a lodge and restaurant. Framed newspaper articles and photographs of famous visitors cover the walls in the lobby hallway. One photo shows a proud Robert Rand next to his trophy catch: a seven-and-a-half-foot, 187-pound tarpon caught in March 1939. Another is of Dwight and Mamie Eisenhower. Dwight is wearing shorts and a scruffy fishing hat. The

Rod and Gun Club

grin on his face and the long rack of fish behind him indicate that he must have had a big day. The lobby is a trophy room. A five-foot-long sawfish bill, a gaping shark's jaw, a stretched alligator hide, deer and wild boar heads, and an assortment of game fish festoon the dark, wood-paneled walls. A stuffed raccoon keeps an eye on guests from its permanent perch behind the registration desk.

The Rod and Gun Club restaurant, in the main lodge, serves seafood and steaks, as well as some Everglades specialties: gator tail and frog legs. The kitchen will also gladly prepare your own fresh catch. Lodging guests stay in spacious duplex cottages adjacent to the lodge.

Another fine lodging option is the Ivey House Bed & Breakfast, with eighteen modern hotel rooms, a cottage, plus eleven more rooms and a restaurant in their restored circa-1928 lodge.

Everglades City may be a sleepy little fishing community with a full-time population of fewer than seven hundred, but there are plenty of activities for visitors. There are really only two seasons here: "mosquito" and "non-mosquito," which roughly coincide with the wet and dry seasons. Non-mosquito/dry season is from December through March. Those who live here year-round are hardy souls indeed, but they live in an amazing, otherworldly place that can be explored by canoe or kayak. One of the best ways to see the back country is on an airboat ride. Two locally owned outfitters, Captain Doug's Airboat Tours and Speedy Johnson's Airboat Rides, have been operating out of Everglades City for decades. Except for those that park rangers use for patrolling, airboats aren't allowed in Everglades National Park. They are, however, allowed in the Big Cypress National Preserve. Everglades City sits on the border between the two, so the airboat tours go north, east, or west.

On the town circle you'll find the Museum of the Everglades in the Historic Laundry Building, restored in 1997. Built as one of Barron Collier's company-town buildings in 1927, it remained a commercial laundry through World War II. In 2001, it was added to the National Register of Historic Places. The museum opened in 1998. A collection of Calusa and Seminole artifacts, as well as old photographs chronicling the town's evolution, are on permanent

Historic Everglades City Hall

display. Also on display here is some of the original laundry equipment dating back to the 1940s, including a giant centrifugal dry cleaner. There are also rotating exhibits of works by local artists, artisans, and photographers.

Highway 29 continues south out of Everglades City down to Chokoloskee Island. Archaeologists tell us that coastal mound dwellers inhabited Chokoloskee and the surrounding islands more than two thousand years ago, possibly as far back as ten thousand years. These inhabitants left relics remarkably similar to those left by Central American Mayans, which has led to speculation that they may have communicated and traded with the Mayans. More recently, Chokoloskee was a refuge for the Seminole Indians forced out of central Florida during the Seminole Wars. Chief Billy Bowlegs lived here in the mid-1800s.

About the same time W. S. Allen was developing Everglades City, Ted Smallwood was settling Chokoloskee. He began farming there in 1896, and in 1906 he turned his home into a trading post that grew into a full-time store and post office. Smallwood traded with the Seminoles, fishermen, fur traders, and other early settlers on the island. By 1917, the store had outgrown his house, so he built a larger facility down on the water's edge. In 1924, a violent storm blew four feet of water into the store and actually shifted its foundation. The following year, he raised the building up on wooden pilings, just in time to weather the severe 1926 hurricane.

In 1974, the Smallwood Store was placed on the National Register of Historic Places. It remained an active store up until 1982. Lynn Smallwood, Ted's granddaughter, owns it now. In 1990, she began restoring the tin-sided, tin-roofed building as a museum.

From the front door, you can see straight through the length of the store to the back door and the porch, which looks out over the water. The interior of the store looks much the same as it did for the better part of the twentieth century. Wall shelves hold staple goods and supplies that were typical of the store's inventory. A life-size likeness of Ted Smallwood sits in his favorite rocking chair. With his bushy mustache, tall hat, and glasses, he could be Teddy Roosevelt's twin. The store's original furnishings are still here. There's a long counter that runs the length of one wall with old books and photographs

Historic Ted Smallwood's Store

from Chokoloskee's bygone era on display. Decades' worth of elbows leaning on the countertop have worn its edge smooth and rounded. One room serves as a memorial to one of this area's most intriguing characters–Totch Brown, who lived near here for three-quarters of a century. He made a living as a fisherman and gator trapper and even admitted to having been an occasional marijuana smuggler in the early 1970s. The store has been restored, but (except for Ted) it is not a re-creation. This is the real thing.

In Chokoloskee I found another one of those great little middle-of-nowhere breakfast-lunch spots: the Havana Café, with some of the best authentic Cuban food this side of west Tampa.

Leaving Everglades City behind, turn east onto Highway 41/ Tamiami Trail and keep an eye out for the Ochopee Post Office about four miles down the road on the right. It's a corrugated tin shed, hardly bigger than an outhouse, and has the distinction of being the smallest official post office in the United States. The tiny building was originally an irrigation pipe shed for a tomato farm. A 1953 fire burned Ochopee's previous general store and post office to the ground. Postmaster Sidney Brown hurriedly put the pipe shed into temporary service. It served its purpose so well that no one

Ochopee Post Office

saw reason to replace it. Tourists stop here regularly just to get the Ochopee 34141 postmark on their mail. Across the road at Joanie's Blue Crab Café, you'll find great Everglades cuisine—gator, frog legs, and soft-shell crab—and live music on weekends.

The Tamiami Trail impacted the Everglades in many ways. Back in the 1930s it revealed some of the mystery of the place to anyone with a Model T. What had once been an expedition to cross the state was now a mere day's drive. What the Trail's constructors had not anticipated was the choking environmental effect it would have. Like the Lake Okeechobee levees, the Trail (and later its cousin to the north, Alligator Alley) was essentially an enormous Everglades-wide dam that halted that almost imperceptible flow of water south. Much work has been done in recent decades to channel water beneath the highways, but it seems to be perhaps too little, too late.

DIRECTIONS: From Highway 41/Tamiami Trail, turn south onto SR 29 (25 miles southeast of Naples) to Everglades City. Continue south another four miles to Chokoloskee. Ochopee is 29 miles southeast of Naples on Highway 41/ Tamiami Trail.

DON'T MISS: Historic Ted Smallwood's Store in Chokoloskee

CARD SOUND

Population: 50

*I*F YOU'RE A CARL HIAASEN FAN (as I am), you'll recognize Card Sound as the place where the villains in Hiaasen's novels sometimes dump the bodies of their victims. So where is it? If you've ever driven from Homestead down to Key West, you may have thought Highway 1/A1A was the only road, but there is a detour, and if you're hungry for some just-caught blue crab, conch fritters, or a grilled mahi or red snapper sandwich, then it's a detour worth taking. On the way out of Homestead, watch for Highway 997/905A Card Sound Road to veer off to the left. Follow it and enjoy the scenery and solitude for the next twelve miles. (Or, if you're coming back from the Keys, turn right on 905 just north of Key Largo.) Right at the base of the Card Sound Bridge you will find the quintessential Florida

Cracker open-air dive bar and grill, Alabama Jack's. It's been there since 1947. Don't be scared off by the rustic appearance. The food's good, and the folks that run it are friendly.

DIRECTIONS: Follow Highway 997/905A Card Sound Road from Homestead, or Highway 905 from Key Largo.

DON'T MISS: Alabama Jack's

STILTSVILLE

Population: 10 (part-time)

*B*ISCAYNE NATIONAL PARK, created in 1980, stretches from the southern tip of Key Biscayne to the northern tip of Key Largo. It is probably the National Park system's most unusual park, in that 95 percent of its 180,000 acres are underwater. Seven-mile-long Elliott Key is its only substantial piece of dry land. Spectacular coral reefs, brimming with tropical sea life, rest just beneath the surface. Lots of exciting history has taken place in these waters. Villainous pirates, including the infamous Black Caesar, who lived on Elliott Key for awhile, frequented these waters in the 1700s. The shallow reefs have been a graveyard for ships as far back as history records. In 1942, a German submarine sank a tanker, killing fourteen men, just offshore from Key Biscayne.

Forty years before Biscayne National Park opened, the first stilt houses went up in the shallow flats of Biscayne Bay, north of Elliott Key. Stiltsville's first "homesteader" was a fisherman named "Crawfish" Eddie Walker. Sometime in the mid-1930s, Crawfish Eddie staked his claim on an abandoned run-aground barge. He built a bait-and-beer shack on one end, and went into business selling to passing fishermen. In 1939, another Eddie—Turner this time—built a bar and restaurant on pilings not far from Crawfish Eddie's called the Quarterdeck Club.

This was the beginning of Stiltsville's wild era. Rumors of unruly parties and debauchery spread. After *Life* magazine ran an article about the Quarterdeck Club in 1941, word was out. Not everybody was happy about it. Some of the new and well-to-do residents of Key Biscayne were displeased about the near-offshore activity. Those protests not withstanding, people began to build weekend fishing cabins on stilts out in the bay in the mid-1940s. The Quarterdeck Club burned in the early 1950s, but others took its place. Harry "Pierre" Churchville opened the Biscayne Bay Bikini Club in 1962 on a grounded one-hundred-fifty-foot yacht. Three years later, Florida State Beverage agents shut it down for operating without a liquor license. Stiltsville mellowed a bit after that.

Up until 1969, the stilt houses stood free of property taxes or rent. That year the State of Florida began charging the "squatters" a property lease fee. Stiltsville had as many as twenty houses in the 1970s. Hurricanes took their toll on some. In the 1980s, the houses numbered in the mid-teens. After Hurricane Andrew blew through in August 1992, only seven were left standing. None can be rebuilt because of National Park restrictions on building or rebuilding residential structures. In fact, those seven remaining houses were scheduled to be destroyed in 1999, despite the fact that Stiltsville's existence predated the creation of Biscayne National Park by four decades. A grassroots group called Save Our Stiltsville staved off the demolition and worked to obtain historical status for Stiltsville; in 2003, the Stiltsville Trust was established to protect the seven remaining houses, with the leaseholders assigned as caretakers to raise funds and preserve the structures.

DIRECTIONS: By boat, travel four to six miles due south of Cape Florida Lighthouse on Key Biscayne.

TAVERNIER, ISLAMORADA

Population: Tavernier 2,173; Islamorada 6,435

*T*HE FLORIDA KEYS SIT ON TOP of the only living coral reef in the continental United States. Here, particularly in the northern "Upper" Keys, visitors find some of the best big-game fishing and scuba diving in the world. It's difficult to get off the beaten path down here since there is only one path from Key Largo south—US Highway 1, also known as the Overseas Highway. However, this makes it easy to give directions using mile markers. Add two digits to the end of the mile marker number and that's the street address.

Three pioneer families—the Russells, the Pinders, and the Parkers—sailed to Upper Matecumbe Key (Islamorada) in the mid- and late-1800s from the Bahamas. These Anglo-Bahamian settlers were called "Conchs," after the shellfish that was such a staple in their diet. They built their homes from driftwood, planted pineapple and Key lime groves, and fished. In 1905, their island outpost became connected with the rest of civilization when Henry Flagler built his railroad through here on its way to Key West. As a result, a few hotels and vacation homes went up on Islamorada. The Tavernier Hotel went up in 1928 in Tavernier (and is still operating), and Flagler built a fishing camp just south, on Long Key.

In 1935 the Upper Keys would become the setting for one of Florida's most terrifying events. On September 1, 1935, locals on the Lower and Upper Matecumbe Keys were boarding up their homes in preparation for a tropical storm that was crossing the Bahamas. Weather forecasters were predicting that it would pass south of Key West, but by the morning of September 2, Labor Day, barometers on the Matecumbe Keys were dropping rapidly. That meant that the storm had veered northeast and was gaining strength.

A few months before, in the summer of 1935, the Veterans Administration had hired 680 unemployed World War I veterans and sent them to the upper Keys to build Highway 1's roadway and bridges. The press referred to them as "bonus-marching veterans" because they had marched on Washington, D.C., to protest that they could not get jobs after returning from the war and thus wanted their war bonuses accelerated. The roadwork veterans were living in three construction camps on Upper and Lower Matecumbe Keys. About two-thirds of them had gone to Miami or Key West for that Labor Day holiday. Those who remained met a horrible fate.

By nightfall, the winds were howling, and it was apparent that this would be a big one. Families huddled in their wood-frame "Conch" bungalows and storm shelters. At 8:30 P.M., the barometer read an all-time Northern hemisphere record-low pressure of 26.35 millibars.

The hurricane cut a swath right through Upper Matecumbe. Winds blew to 260 miles per hour. A twenty-foot-tall tidal wave swept over the islands, ripping whole houses, with families in them, off their foundations. Roger Albury and his nine family members were in their eight-room Tavernier house when the wave picked it up and carried it over two hundred feet.

Seventeen-year-old Bernard Russell and his family sought shelter in his father's Islamorada lime packinghouse. When flood waters came pouring in, they tried to escape to higher ground. Clinging desperately to each other, they pushed out of the packinghouse and were instantly blown apart. Bernard's sister and his young nephew were torn from his hands. Of the sixty members of the extended Russell family, only eleven survived the hurricane.

Earlier in the day, an eleven-car passenger train had left Miami to try to evacuate the upper Keys residents and WWI-veteran road workers who were working there. The train reached Islamorada right when a wall of water struck, blasting each of the one-hundred-ton passenger cars right off the tracks. Only the locomotive remained upright. It was the last train to travel these tracks; Flagler never rebuilt his railroad.

Ultimately, 408 bodies were counted, but the actual death toll was probably twice that. All of the war-veteran road workers who had stayed on the islands were killed. Months after the storm, remains of victims' bodies were still being recovered. Thirty years later, while dredging on an outlying key near Islamorada, a developer found an automobile with 1935 license plates and five skeletons inside.

In the Islamorada–Helen Wadley Branch Library archives, I found a scathing newspaper editorial entitled "Who Murdered the Vets?" written on September 17, 1935, by Ernest Hemingway. Hemingway was living in Key West at the time and had gone to the upper Keys with crews to assist in the rescue efforts two days after the disaster. His article was an angry indictment of the newly formed Veterans Administration for sending the veterans down to the Keys to work during the most dangerous time of year—hurricane season. It reads in part, "Fishermen such as President Herbert Hoover, and President Roosevelt, do not come to the Florida Keys in hurricane months. . . . There is a known danger to property. . . . But veterans, especially the bonus-marching variety, are not property. They are only human beings; unsuccessful human beings, and all they have to lose are their lives. They are doing coolie labor, for a top wage of $45 a month, and they have been put down on the Florida Keys where they can't make trouble."

The long and painful process of rebuilding began immediately after the storm had passed and the bodies were buried. Young Bernard Russell, who had seen his family all but wiped out, remained on the island. He started his own cabinet-building/carpentry business and later founded Islamorada's first fire rescue department. In a 1991 *St. Petersburg Times* interview, he said, "The thing I have always asked myself is this: 'Why was I spared? Why am I still here?' I saw great big robust he-men, dead on the ground. I saw little skinny children who survived. How do you put that together in your mind? I have to think the Lord might have a purpose for me. I might be needed."

At mile marker 81.8 you will find the 1935 Hurricane Monument. It's also a tomb that contains the cremated remains of some of the storm's victims. A plaque at the base of the twelve-foot-tall coral keystone monolith reads, "Dedicated to the memory of the civilians and war veterans whose lives were lost in the hurricane of September Second 1935."

Entrance to the historic Cheeca Lodge grounds is right next door (at mile marker 82) to the Hurricane Monument. Original owner Clara Downey called it the Olney Inn (after her hometown, Olney, Maryland) when she opened in 1946. There were just twenty-two cottages then. One of the Olney Inn's first guests was President Harry Truman, whose stay set the stage for the resort to become a popular retreat for politicians, sports figures, and movie stars for decades to come. The name changed to Cheeca Lodge in the 1960s, when Cynthia and Carl Twitchell purchased it and added the lodge, oceanfront villas, and a golf course. "Chee" was Cynthia's nickname and the "ca" came from "Carl." In 2005 the current owners, the Johnson family, did a $30 million renovation, and in 2009 they rebuilt the main lodge.

Among the first buildings that the original Conchs built on Islamorada was a church (1890) and a schoolhouse (1900), on property that is now part of the Cheeca Lodge compound. Next to the church, they established a small cemetery. The 1935 hurricane destroyed the schoolhouse and the church, but the Pioneer Cemetery remains. Looking out of place among the beach loungers and rental Hobie Cats, the tiny cemetery is surrounded by a low, white picket fence. Only eleven gravesites are marked, but there are more without names. In the center, a life-size statue of an angel marks the grave of Etta Dolores Pinder (1899–1914). Tossed a thousand feet in the mighty winds of the 1935 hurricane, the angel, with one wing broken

1935 Hurricane Monument

and a hand missing, nevertheless stands tall. A historical marker in one corner of the cemetery reads: "This cemetery memorializes the determination and vision of over fifty pioneer Anglo-Bahamian Conchs who labored to settle and organize the first community on Matecumbe Key. Descendants of three pioneer families, the Russells who homesteaded in 1854, the Pinders in 1873, and the Parkers in 1898, are buried on this land."

Another, more recent, piece of Islamorada history can be found just south of the cemetery, at mile marker 81.2. In 1947, Sid and Roxie Siderious purchased a little place built in 1928 called the Rustic Inn, which they opened as a roadside diner called the Green Turtle Inn. They specialized in locally fished turtle made into soups and steaks. At that time, sea turtles were plentiful in the Keys, but within a few short decades, their population was decimated. Fishing for sea turtles was finally outlawed in the 1970s. Now the restaurant serves freshwater turtle bought from turtle farms near Lake Okeechobee.

I've had the Green Turtle Inn's turtle soup and it is tasty. I also like their conch salad, which comes in a tomato-based marinade with onions and green and red peppers. Conch, a large mollusk native to these waters, is Florida's answer to California's abalone. In 2006 the Green Turtle Inn underwent a major post–Hurricane Wilma renovation.

DIRECTIONS: Tavernier is 67 miles south of Miami on US Highway 1. Continue 12 more miles south to Islamorada.

DON'T MISS: The Pioneer Cemetery on the grounds of the Cheeca Lodge

BIG PINE KEY

Population: 5,032

*B*IG PINE KEY, the largest island in the lower keys,
could be Florida's answer to the Galapagos Islands. Along with its
northwest appendage, No Name Key, it is home to a number of rare
and endangered birds, reptiles, and mammals—including the seldom-
sighted, short-eared Lower Keys marsh rabbit (rumored to actually
swim between the islands occasionally). Big Pine Key's best known
and most endangered inhabitant is the petite Key, or toy, deer. Key
deer are the smallest race of North American deer and are indigenous
to the Lower Keys; nearly the entire population is found on Big Pine
and No Name keys. A typical adult weighs between forty and seventy
pounds and stands less than two and a half feet tall at the shoulder.
Disproportionately large ears and brown eyes add considerably to the

deer's "cuteness" quotient. Unfortunately, their adorableness may be one of the factors contributing to their demise.

For the most part, commercial development did not come to Big Pine Key until the late 1960s, but there had been small settlements here and on No Name Key for over a hundred years. Some of the people who lived here in the mid-1800s were fishermen and spongers, but most came to harvest buttonwood trees–found in the lower and wetter areas of the island–for charcoal. Key West, thirty miles south, was at the height of its wreckers "Golden Era," and Big Pine Key charcoal was much in demand as a fuel source. But nothing lasts forever. At the end of the nineteenth century, with the construction of lighthouses in the Lower Keys to warn ships away from reefs, the wrecking industry died a quick death. Big Pine Key's buttonwood charcoal business soon followed suit.

In 1905, Henry Flagler started building his Overseas Railroad and began connecting the dots of the Keys. It rolled across Big Pine Key in 1911 and finished in Key West in 1912. The Labor Day Hurricane of 1935–the largest ever to strike Florida–brought an end to the Overseas Railroad when it ripped across the Upper Keys, blasting an entire train, sent by Flagler to rescue road workers on Islamorada, right off the tracks. (See the Tavernier and Islamorada chapter.)

By 1938, the Overseas Highway had been paved to Key West, reusing many of Flagler's railway bridges, but Big Pine Key and No Name Key were largely unaffected. The islands' few inhabitants were mostly fishermen or rumrunners left over from the Prohibition era and seeking anonymity.

In 1957, the U. S. Fish and Wildlife Service established the National Key Deer Refuge on Big Pine and No Name keys. Hunters had decimated the Key deer population: There were fewer than fifty deer in 1949. First refuge manager and local hero Jack Watson fought passionately for their survival and is credited with saving them, almost single-handedly, from extinction. He battled poachers like the sheriff in a Wild West town, sometimes resorting to sinking their boats and torching their pickup trucks. Watson retired in 1975, and three years later the Key deer reached a population peak of four hundred.

Sadly, those numbers declined over the subsequent two decades. Loss of habitat, unusually low birth rates (Key deer rarely have multiple births), and automobile strikes are the reasons cited most often. When I visited Big Pine Key and No Name Key in 1998, there were fewer than three hundred deer left on the islands (counted in 1997). Recently, however, there has been significant progress in the effort to bolster the Key deer's population. The most recent count puts their numbers at over six hundred. Despite this improvement, they are still at great risk. More than half of those that die each year are killed by automobile strikes. Hand-feeding exacerbates the problem. These little guys are so cute that people get out of their cars to feed them. The deer are quick learners, and before long they start running out to cars, and invariably get hit. The fine for feeding a Key deer is $250.

Publicizing the National Key Deer Refuge is a double-edged sword: the value of increased awareness of the Key deer's plight, weighed against the potential for more traffic. Every person I've spoken to in the community has said something to me about driving slowly and carefully (whether I asked about it or not). The local police do their part. They write speeding tickets for just one mile per hour over the limit, which is 35 M.P.H. almost everywhere on the islands.

Big Pine Key is decidedly quieter and more leisurely than its famous neighbor to the south. An interesting and eclectic place to stay is the Barnacle Bed & Breakfast, where leisure has been refined to an art form. Long Beach Road dead-ends a short ways past it, so there is no traffic. A simple limestone wall marks the entrance. The Barnacle is an architectural enigma. Its style doesn't fall neatly into any conventional category. Modern, eclectic, nautical, tropical—there are no right angles. Its pipe railings, archways, and generous open-air balcony remind me, more than anything else, of an ocean liner, albeit with an exterior painted in varying shades of earth tones reminiscent of the 1970s. From the top-floor sunrise-watching deck (the ocean liner's bow), guests can scan the Atlantic's vivid turquoise water for rolling dolphin or maybe a jumping manta ray.

Original owner Steven "Woody" Cornell designed and built the Barnacle in 1976. Dive operators Tim and Jane Marquis bought it from Woody in 1994. I stayed in their downstairs Ocean Room (done in shades of pastel sea green and plum), which opened directly onto the beach. Multicolored hexagonal tiles covered the floor. Creative use of space for the bathroom, the kitchenette, and shelving reminded me of a stateroom on the *Queen Elizabeth*. Again, the walls were skewed at odd angles, and the floor plan was a series of triangles. The bed sat in its own little alcove that faced the coconut palm–lined beach and the ocean, which I could gaze out at through sliding glass doors. As of 2010 the Barnacle has new owners again–Debi and Jason–and all reports indicate that they are doing a great job.

A likely place to spot wildlife is Big Pine Key's Blue Hole. Back in the 1930s, road construction crews mined the hard oolitic limestone that makes up Big Pine Key. They extracted most of what they needed from one quarry near the center of the island, a place now called the Blue Hole. It's one of the few spots in all the Lower Keys where a substantial amount of fresh rainwater collects, and it is a crucial source of drinking water for the island's wildlife, particularly the Key deer. Highway 940, also called Key Deer Boulevard, cuts a northern path through hardwood hammocks and pinelands, bisecting the largest of the designated Key Deer Refuge areas. The Blue Hole is just off 940 on the left, a mile and a quarter from Highway 1.

A short loop trail leads into the hammock from the back side of the Blue Hole. I am impressed at how determined the plant life is

Barnacle Bed & Breakfast

around here. Buttonwood, palmetto, slash pines (for which Big Pine Key was named), and gumbo-limbo trees grow right out of the rock with virtually no topsoil. A variety of orchids and air plants use both living and fallen trees as hosts.

This is a good place to see a Key deer, as is No Name Key, particularly around sunset. The first time I saw one was on No Name Key. It was a doe about the size of a springer spaniel. She sauntered across the road up ahead of me, stopped for a moment to scratch one of her oversize ears with a hind hoof, took an uninterested glance at me, then trotted off into the woods.

On your way to No Name Key (follow the signs up Wilder Road), stop in at the No Name Pub, just on the Big Pine Key side of the bridge over to No Name Key. Watch carefully for it on the left. Mangroves and cactus half conceal the clapboard building, but a hand-painted sign nailed to a palm tree tells you it's there.

Built in 1936, the No Name Pub was originally a Cuban trading post and general store. It is also reputed to have been a smuggler's hangout/hideout and a brothel. Since the mid-1970s, it's been a bar and restaurant, the oldest on the island. Inside, the No Name Pub upholds the Keys' dive-bar-decor tradition of signed and dated dollar bills stapled all over the walls and ceiling. Patrons have also carved their initials in the bar, which was built from salvaged scrap from the old wooden No Name Key bridge (which was replaced with a sturdier concrete crossing). This place also has some of the best pizza in the Keys.

DIRECTIONS: Drive thirty-five miles north of Key West on Highway A1A.

DON'T MISS: The No Name Pub

APPENDIX

North Region

Milton and Bagdad

Arcadia Mill Site Museum
5709 Mill Pond Road
Milton, Florida 32583
(850) 626-4433
www.historicpensacola.org/arcadia.cfm

Bagdad Village Preservation Association
Museum
4512 Church Street
Bagdad, Florida 32530
(850) 626-0985
www.bagdadvillage.org

Santa Rosa Chamber of Commerce
5247 Stewart Street
Milton, Florida 32570
(850) 623-2339
www.srcchamber.com

Santa Rosa Historical Society
6866 Caroline Street
Milton, Florida 32570
(850) 626-9830
www.santarosahistoricalsociety.com

West Florida Railroad Museum
206 Henry Street
Milton, Florida 32570
(850) 623-3645
www.wfrm.org

DeFuniak Springs

Big Store
782 Baldwin Avenue
DeFuniak Springs, Florida 32435
(850) 892-7008

Bookstore
640 Baldwin Avenue
DeFuniak Springs, Florida 32435
(850) 892-3119

Busy Bee Cafe
35 South 7th Street
DeFuniak Springs, Florida 32435
(850) 892-6700

Hotel DeFuniak
400 US Highway 90 East
DeFuniak Springs, Florida 32433
(850) 892-4383
www.hoteldefuniak.com

Little Big Store
35 South 8th Street
DeFuniak Springs, Florida 32435
(850) 892-6066

Murray's Café
660 Baldwin Avenue
DeFuniak Springs, Florida 32435
(850) 951-9941
www.murrayscafe.com

Southeby's Antiques Gallery
27 Crescent Drive
DeFuniak Springs, Florida 32435
(850) 892-6292
www.defuniakspringsfl.com/southebys_
antiques.htm

Walton County Heritage Museum
DeFuniak Springs Depot
1140 Circle Drive
DeFuniak Springs, Florida 32435
(850) 951-2127
www.waltoncountyheritage.org/museum.
htm

Walton-DeFuniak Public Library
3 Circle Drive
DeFuniak Springs, Florida 32435
(850) 892-3624

Two Egg
Lawrence Grocery
3972 Highway 69A/Wintergreen Road
Two Egg, Florida 32443

Quincy
Allison House Inn
215 North Madison Street
Quincy, Florida 32351
(850) 875-2511
(888) 904-2511
www.allisonhouseinn.com

Gadsden Arts Center
Bell & Bates Hardware Store Building
13 North Madison Street
Quincy, Florida 32351
(850) 875-4866
www.gadsdenarts.org

McFarlin House Bed & Breakfast Inn
305 East King Street
Quincy, Florida 32351
(850) 875-2526
(877) 370-4701
www.mcfarlinhouse.com

Quincy Music Theatre
Leaf Theatre Building
118 East Washington Street
Quincy, Florida 32351
(850) 875-9444
www.qmtonline.com

Havana
H & H Furniture and Design
302 North Main Street
Havana, Florida 32333
(850) 539-6886
www.havanaflorida.com/H-and-H.aspx

Joanie's Gourmet Café Market and
Fabulous Café
102 West 8th Street
Havana, Florida 32333
(850) 539-4433
www.havanaflorida.com/Joanie-Gourmet-
Market.aspx

Little River General Store
308 North Main Street
Havana, Florida 32333
(850) 539-6900
www.havanaflorida.com/Little-River-
General-Store.aspx

McLauchlin House
201 South Seventh Avenue
Havana, Florida 32333
(850) 539-3333

Mirror Image Antiques
303 First Street NW
Havana, Florida 32333
(850) 539-7422
www.havanaflorida.com/Mirror-Image-
Antiques.aspx

Tomato Café
107 West 7th Avenue
Havana, Florida 32333
(850) 539-2285
www.havanaflorida.com/Tomato-Cafe.
aspx

Fernandina Beach
29 South
29 South 3rd Street
Fernandina Beach, Florida 32034
(904) 277-7919
www.29southrestaurant.com

Addison on Amelia Bed & Breakfast
614 Ash Street
Fernandina Beach, Florida 32034
(904) 277-1604
(800) 943-1604
www.addisononamelia.com

Amelia Island Museum of History
233 South 3rd Street
Fernandina Beach, Florida 32034
(904) 261-7378
www.ameliamuseum.org

Beech Street Grill
801 Beech Street
Fernandina Beach, Florida 32034
(904) 277-3663
www.beechstreetgrill.com

Book Loft Bookstore
214 Centre Street
Fernandina Beach, Florida 32034
(904) 261-8991

Books Plus
107 Centre Street
Fernandina Beach, Florida 32034
(904) 261-0303
www.booksplusamelia.com

Elizabeth Pointe Lodge
98 South Fletcher Avenue
Fernandina Beach, Florida 32034
(904) 277-4851
(800) 772-3359
www.elizabethpointelodge.com

Fairbanks House Bed & Breakfast
227 South 7th Street
Fernandina Beach, Florida 32034
(904) 277-0500
(888) 891-9882
www.fairbankshouse.com

Florida House Inn
22 South 3rd Street
Fernandina Beach, Florida 32034
(904) 491-3322
(800) 258-3301
www.floridahouseinn.com

Fort Clinch State Park
2601 Atlantic Avenue
Fernandina Beach, Florida 32034
(904) 277-7274
www.floridastateparks.org/fortclinch

Hunt's Art and Artifacts Gallery
316 Centre Street
Fernandina Beach, Florida 32034
(904) 261-8225

Joe's 2nd Street Bistro
14 South 2rd Street
Fernandina Beach, Florida 32034
(904) 321-2558
www.joesbistro.com

Palace Saloon
117 Centre Street
Fernandina Beach, Florida 32034
(904) 491-3332
www.thepalacesaloon.com

Patty Cakes Bakery
3 North 4th Street
Fernandina Beach, Florida 32034
(904) 310-6599
www.pattycakesflorida.com

Seaside

Bud & Alley's Restaurant
Beachside/Cinderella Circle
Seaside, Florida 32459
(850) 231-5900
www.budandalleys.com

Inn by the Sea, Vera Bradley
38 Seaside Avenue
Seaside, Florida 32459
(800) 358-8696
(850) 231-1940
Dining: (800) 591-8696
www.cottagerentalagency.com/
InnbytheSea.asp

Keramikos
306 Ruskin Place
Seaside, Florida 32459
(850) 231-5564

Modica Market
Central Square
Seaside, Florida 32459
(850) 231-1214
www.modicamarket.com

Newbill Collection
309 Ruskin Place
Seaside, Florida 32459
(850) 231-4500

Pickles Beachside Grill
Beachside/Piazza Nancy Drew
Seaside, Florida 32459
(850) 231-5686
www.sweetwilliamsltd.com/pickles.html

Seaside Cottage Rental Agency
P.O. Box 4730
Seaside, Florida 32459
(800) 277-8696
www.cottagerentalagency.com

Seaside Motor Court
Seaside, Florida 32459
(800) 277-8696
www.cottagerentalagency.com/cottages1.asp

Seaside Repertory Theatre
P.O. Box 4814
Seaside, Florida 32459
(850) 231-3033
www.seasiderep.org

Studio 210
210 Ruskin Place
Seaside, Florida 32459
(850) 231-3720

Sundog Books
89 Central Square
Seaside, Florida 32459
(850) 231-5481
www.sundogbooks.com

Apalachicola, St. George Island, and Carrabelle

Apalachicola Seafood Grill
100 Market Street
Apalachicola, Florida 32320
(850) 653-9510

Boss Oyster Restaurant
123 Water Street
Apalachicola, Florida 32320
(850) 653-9364
www.apalachicolariverinn.com/boss.html

Carrabelle Junction
88 Tallahassee Street
Carrabelle, Florida 32322
(850) 697-9550

Chef Eddie's Magnolia Grill
99 11th Street
Apalachicola, Florida 32320
(850) 653-8000

Collins Vacation Rentals
60 East Gulf Beach Drive
St. George Island, Florida 32328
(800) 683-9776
www.collinsvacationrentals.com

Consulate Suites
76 Water Street
Apalachicola, Florida 32320
(800) 341-2021
(850) 927-2282
www.consulatesuites.com

Coombs House Inn B & B
80 6th Street
Apalachicola, Florida 32320
(850) 653-9199
www.coombshouseinn.com

Eddy Teach's Raw Bar
37 East Pine Street
St. George Island, Florida 32328
(850) 927-5050
www.eddyteachs.com

Gibson Inn
51 Avenue C
Apalachicola, Florida 32320
(850) 653-2191
www.gibsoninn.com

Grady Market
76 Water Street
Apalachicola, Florida 32320
(850) 653-4099
www.gradymarket.com

John Gorrie State Museum
P.O. Box 267
Corner of 6th Street and Avenue D
Apalachicola, Florida 32320
(850) 653-9347
www.floridastateparks.org/
johngorriemuseum/default.cfm

Julian G. Bruce/St. George Island State
Park
St. George Island, Florida 32328
(850) 927-2111
www.floridastateparks.org/stgeorgeisland/
default.cfm

Old Time Soda Fountain
93 Market Street
Apalachicola, Florida 32320
(850) 653-2606

Owl Café
15 Avenue D
Apalachicola, Florida 32320
(850) 653-9888
www.owlcafeflorida.com

Resort Vacation Properties
140 West 1st Street
St. George Island, Florida 32328
(850) 927-2322
(877) 272-8206 toll free
www.resortvacationproperties.com

St. George Island Lighthouse Museum
and Visitor Center
2 East Gulf Beach Drive
St. George Island, Florida 32328
(850) 927-7744
(888) 927-7744
www.stgeorgelight.org
www.seestgeorgeisland.com

Tamara's Floridita Café
71 Market Street
Apalachicola, Florida 32320
(850) 653-4111
www.tamarascafe.com

That Place In Apalach Restaurant
17 Avenue E
Apalachicola, Florida 32320
(850) 653-9898
www.thatplaceinapalach.com

Wakulla Springs
Edward Ball Wakulla Springs State Park
and Lodge
550 Wakulla Park Drive
Wakulla Springs, Florida 32327
 (850) 926-0700
www.floridastateparks.org/wakullasprings

St. Marks and Sopchoppy
Backwoods Pizza & Bistro
106 Municipal Avenue
Sopchoppy, Florida 32358
(850) 962-2220

Riverside Café
69 Riverside Drive
St. Marks, Florida 32355
(850) 925-5668
www.riversidebay.com

Sopchoppy Worm Gruntin' Festival (2nd
weekend in April)
P.O. Box 272
Sopchoppy, Florida 32358
(850) 962-4138
www.wormgruntinfestival.com
(850) 962-4138

St. Marks National Wildlife Refuge
1255 Lighthouse Road
St. Marks, FL 32355
(850) 925-6121
www.fws.gov/saintmarks

St. Marks Smokehouse and Oyster Bar
56 Riverside Drive
St. Marks, Florida 32355
(850) 925-7727
www.riversidebay.com/210.html

Sweet Magnolia Inn Bed & Breakfast
803 Port Leon Drive
St. Marks, Florida 32355
(850) 925-7670
www.sweetmagnolia.com

Jasper
H & F Restaurant
202 Hatley Street
Jasper, Florida 32052
(386) 792-3074

White Springs
American Canoe Adventures
10315 South East141st Boulevard
White Springs, Florida 32096
(386) 397-1309
www.aca1.com

Florida Folk Festival (4th weekend in May)
www.floridafolkfestival.com
(877) 635-3655

Nature & Heritage Tourism Center
Corner of Highway 136 and Highway 41
White Springs, Florida 32096
(386) 397-4461

Stephen Foster State Folk Culture Center/
State Park
U. S. Highway 41 North
White Springs, Florida 32096
(386) 397-2733
www.floridastateparks.org/stephenfoster

Telford Hotel, Bed & Breakfast,
Restaurant
16521 River Street
White Springs, Florida 32096
(386) 397-2000
www.telfordhotel.net

White Springs Bed & Breakfast
16630 Spring Street
White Springs, Florida 32096
(386) 397-4252
www.whitespringsbnb.com

Keaton Beach and Dekle Beach
Keaton Beach Hot Dog Stand
21239 Keaton Beach Drive
Keaton Beach, Florida 32348
(850) 578-2164

Steinhatchee
Steinhatchee Landing Resort
P.O. Box 789
228 Highway 51 North
Steinhatchee, Florida 32359
(352) 498-3513
(800) 584-1709
www.steinhatcheelanding.com

High Springs
Blue Springs
7450 NE 60th Street
(off County Road 340)
High Springs, Florida 32643
(386) 454-1369
www.bluespringspark.com

Burch Antiques Too
60 North Main Street
High Springs, Florida 32643
(386) 454-1500

Ginnie Springs
7300 Ginnie Springs Road
High Springs, Florida 32643
(386) 454-7188
www.ginniespringsoutdoors.com

Grady House Bed & Breakfast
420 North West 1st Avenue
High Springs, Florida 32643
(386) 454-2206
www.gradyhouse.com

Great Outdoors Restaurant and Trading
Company
High Springs Historic Opera House
65 Main Street
High Springs, Florida 32643
(386) 454-1288
www.greatoutdoorsdining.com

Heart Strings Antiques
215 North Main Street
High Springs, Florida 32643
(386) 454-4081

High Springs Antiques Center
145 North Main Street
High Springs, Florida 32643
(386) 454-4770

Ichetucknee Springs State Park
12087 SW Highway 27
Fort White, Florida 32038
(386) 497-2511
www.ichetucknee-springs.com

Poe Springs Park
28800 North West 182nd Avenue
High Springs, Florida 32643
(386) 454-1992
www.naturequest-usa.com

Rustic Inn Bed & Breakfast
15529 NW State Road 45
High Springs, Florida 32643
(386) 454-1223
www.rusticinn.net

Santa Fe River Canoe Outpost
2025 NW Santa Fe Boulevard
High Springs, Florida 32643
(386) 454-2050
www.santaferiver.com

Wisteria Cottage (antiques)
225 North Main Street
High Springs, Florida 32643
(386) 454-8447

Cross Creek, Evinston, Micanopy, and McIntosh
Antique Deli
Highway 441 and Avenue G
McIntosh, Florida 32664
(352) 591-1436

Garage at Micanopy
212 NE Cholokka Boulevard
Micanopy, Florida 32667
(352) 466-0614

Herlong Mansion Bed & Breakfast
402 NE Cholokka Boulevard
Micanopy, Florida 32667
(352) 466-3322
(800) 437-5664
www.herlong.com

Marjorie Kinnan Rawlings State Historic
Site
18700 CR 325
Cross Creek
www.floridastateparks.org/
marjoriekinnanrawlings/
(352) 466-3672

McIntosh 1890s Festival
Friends of McIntosh, Incorporated
P.O. Box 436
McIntosh, Florida 32664
(352) 591-4038
www.friendsofmcintosh.org

McIntosh Railroad Depot Historical
Museum
East End of Avenue G
McIntosh, Florida 32664
(352) 591-4038
www.friendsofmcintosh.com

Micanopy Historical Society Museum
607 NE Cholokka Boulevard
Micanopy, FL 32667
(352) 466-3200
www.afn.org/~micanopy

O. Brisky Books
NE Cholokka Boulevard
PO Box 585
Micanopy, Florida 32667
(352) 466-3910

Old Florida Café
203 Northeast Cholokka Boulevard
Micanopy, Florida 32667
(352) 466-3663

Rocky's Villa Diner
18505 U. S. Highway 441
McIntosh, Florida 32664
(352) 591-1809

Wood & Swink Store and Post Office
18320 SE CR 225
Evinston, Florida 32633
(352) 591-4100

Yearling Restaurant
14531 East CR 325
Cross Creek/Hawthorne, Florida 32640
(352) 466-3999
www.yearlingrestaurant.net

Crescent City and Welaka
Andersen's Lodge
10 Boston Street
Welaka, Florida 32193
(386) 467-3344

Floridian Sports Club
P.O. Box 730
Welaka, Florida 32193
(386) 467-2181

Sprague House Bed & Breakfast
125 Central Avenue
Crescent City, Florida 32112
(386) 698-2622
www.spraguehouse.com

Cedar Key
Cedar Key Bed & Breakfast
810 3rd Street
Cedar Key, FL 32625
(352) 543-9000
(877) 543-5051
www.cedarkeybandb.com

Cedar Key Historical Society Museum
2nd Street and State Road 24
Cedar Key, Florida 32625
(352) 543-5549
www.cedarkeymuseum.org

Cedar Key State Museum
12231 SW 166th Court
Cedar Key, Florida 32625
(352) 543-5350
www.floridastateparks.org/
cedarkeymuseum

Cedar Keyhole Artist Co-op and Gallery
457 2nd Street
Cedar Key, Florida 32625
(352) 543-5801
www.cedarkeyhole.com

Harbour Master Suites
390 Dock Street
(352) 543-9320
Cedar Key, Florida 32625
www.cedarkeyharbourmaster.com

Island Hotel
373 2nd Street
Cedar Key, Florida 32625
(352) 543-5111
(800) 432-4640
www.islandhotel-cedarkey.com

Sawgrass Motel
471 Dock Street
Cedar Key, Florida 32625
(352) 543-5007

Tony's Seafood Restaurant
597 2nd Street
(352) 543-0022
Cedar Key, Florida 32625
www.tonyschowder.com

Rosewood
Historical marker, Highway 24, eight
miles east of Cedar Key
www.displaysforschools.com/rosewoodrp.
html

Central Region

Yankeetown
Izaak Walton Lodge
1 63rd Street
Yankeetown, Florida 34498
Developers' website:
www.izaakwaltonlodge.com
Save Yankeetown website:
www.saveyankeetown.com

Dunnellon
Abigail's Café & Coffee Shop
20607 West Pennsylvania Avenue
Dunnellon, Florida 34431
(352) 489-1818

K. P. Hole Park
SW 190th Avenue
Dunnellon, Florida 34432
(352) 489-3055
www.marioncountyfl.org/Parks/PR_
Parks/PR_KP_Hole_Main.htm

Rainbow Springs State Park
19158 SW 81st Place
Dunnellon, Florida 34432
(352) 465-8555
www.floridastateparks.org/rainbowsprings

Oklawaha
Gator Joe's Beach Bar and Grill
12431 SE 135th Avenue
Oklawaha, Florida 32183
(352) 288-3100
www.gatorjoesocala.com

Cassadaga and Lake Helen
Cassadaga Camp Bookstore
1112 Stevens Street
Cassadaga, Florida 32706
(386) 228-2880

Cassadaga Hotel
355 Cassadaga Road
Cassadaga, Florida 32706
(386) 228-2323
www.cassadagahotel.net

Lake Helen Library
221 North Euclid Avenue
Lake Helen, Florida 32744
(386) 228-1152

Lost In Time Cafe
355 Cassadaga Road
Cassadaga, Florida 32706
(386) 228-2323
www.cassadagahotel.net/cafe.htm

Mount Dora
Adora Inn Bed & Breakfast
610 North Tremain Street
Mount Dora, Florida 32757
(352) 735-3110
www.adorainn.com

Gables Restaurant
322 Alexander Street
Mount Dora, Florida 32757
(352) 383-8993
www.mountdora.com/gables

Goblin Market Restaurant
330 Dora Drawdy Way
Mount Dora, Florida 32757
(352) 735-0059
www.goblinmarketrestaurant.com

Lakeside Inn
100 North Alexander Street
Mount Dora, Florida 32757
(352) 383-4101
(800) 556-5016
www.lakeside-inn.com

Magnolia Inn Bed & Breakfast
347 East Third Avenue
Mount Dora, Florida 32757
(352) 735-3800
(800) 776-2112
www.magnoliainn.net

Piglet's Pantry Dog Bakery
400 North Donnelly Street
Mount Dora, Florida 32757
(352) 735-9779
www.pigletspantry.com

Pisces Rising
239 West 4th Avenue
Mount Dora, Florida 32757
(352) 385-2669
www.piscesrisingdining.com

Segway of Central Florida
140 West 5th Avenue
Mount Dora, Florida 32757
(352) 383-9900
www.segwayofcentralflorida.com

Thee Clockmaker's Shoppe
110 West 5th Avenue
Mount Dora, Florida 32757
(352) 735-5200
www.theeclockmakershoppe.com

Windsor Rose English Tea Room
142 West 4th Avenue
Mount Dora, Florida 32757
(352) 735-2551
www.windsorrose-tearoom.com

Lake Wales
Bok Tower Gardens
1151 Tower Boulevard
Lake Wales, Florida 33853
(863) 676-1408
www.boktowergardens.org

Chalet Suzanne Country Inn and
Restaurant
3800 Chalet Suzanne Drive
Lake Wales, Florida 33859
(863) 676-6011
(800) 433-6011
www.chaletsuzanne.com

Coqui Taino
229 East Stuart Avenue
Lake Wales, Florida 33853
(863) 241-7690

Spook Hill
North Wales Drive at Wilshire Avenue
Lake Wales, Florida 33853

Très Jolie
207 East Park Avenue
Lake Wales, Florida 33853
(863) 676-4142
www.tresjolieltd.com

Inverness
Angelo's Pizzeria
108 West Main Street
Inverness, Florida 34450
(352) 341-0056
www.angelospizzeriaonline.com

Coach's Pub & Eatery
114 West Main Street
Inverness, Florida 34450
(352) 344-3333
www.coachspubandeatery.com

Old Courthouse Heritage Museum
One Courthouse Square
Inverness, Florida 34450
(352) 341-6429
www.cccourthouse.org/courthouse.html

Stumpknockers Restaurant
110 West Main Street
Inverness, Florida 34450
(352) 726-2212
www.stumpknockers.net

Withlacoochee State Trail
315 North Apopka Avenue
Inverness, FL 34450
(352) 726-2251
http://www.dep.state.fl.us/gwt/guide/
regions/crossflorida/trails/with_state.htm

**Floral City, Pineola, Istachatta, and
Nobleton**
Floral City Heritage Hall Museum and
Country Store
8394 East Orange Avenue
Floral City, Florida 34436
Museum: (352) 860-0101
Country Store: (352) 726-7740
www.floralcityhc.com

Istachatta General Store
28198 Istachatta Road/Lingle Road
Istachatta, Florida 34636
(352) 544-1017

Nobleton Outpost Boat Rental
29295 Lake Lindsey Road
Nobleton, Florida 34661
(352) 796-7176
www.nobletonoutpost.com

Aripeka, Bayport, Chassahowitzka, and Ozello
Bayport Park
4140 Cortez Boulevard
Bayport, Florida 34429

Chassahowitzka Hotel
8551 West Miss Maggie Drive
Chassahowitzka, Florida 34448
(352) 382-2075
www.chazhotel.com

Chassahowitzka River Campground and
Recreational Area
8600 West Miss Maggie Drive
Chassahowitzka, Florida 34448
(352) 382-2200
www.citruscountyfl.org/commserv/
commrec/parksrec/chass_camp/
campground.htm

Norfleet's Bait and Tackle Store
Pasco County Road 595
Aripeka, Florida 34679

Peck's Old Port Cove Seafood Restaurant
and Blue Crab Farm
139 North Ozello Trail
Ozello, Florida 34429
(352) 795-2806

Webster
Sumter County Farmers Market/Webster
Flea Market
Corner of Third Street and Highway 471
Webster, Florida 33597
(352) 793-2021
www.sumtercountyfarmersmarket.com

Trilby and Lacoochee
George and Gladys' Bar-B-Q
19215 US Highway 301
Lacoochee, Florida 33523
(352) 567-6229

Little Brown Church of the South
37504 County Road 575
Trilby, FL
(352) 583-2577

Dade City
Church Street Antiques
14117 8th Street
Dade City, Florida 33525
(352) 523-2422

Lunch on Limoges Restaurant
14139 South 7th Street
Dade City, Florida 33525
www.lunchonlimoges.com
(352) 567-5685

Mallie Kyla's Café
American Eagle Antique Mall
14232 7th St.
Dade City, Florida 33525
www.malliekylas.com
(352) 521-3051

Picket Fence
37843 Meridian Avenue
Dade City, Florida 33525
(352) 523-1653

Pioneer Florida Museum
15602 Pioneer Museum Road
Dade City, Florida 33526
(352) 567-0262
www.pioneerfloridamuseum.org

Sugar Creek Too Antiques
14148 8th Street
Dade City, Florida 33525
(352) 567-7712

Christmas
Christmas Post Office
United States Postal Service
23580 East Colonial Drive (State Road 50)
Christmas, Florida 32709-9998
(407) 568-2941

Fort Christmas Historical Park
1300 Fort Christmas Road (SR 420)
Christmas, Florida 32709
(407) 568-4149

Yeehaw Junction
Desert Inn
5540 South Kenansville Road
Intersection of Highway 441 and State
Road 60
Yeehaw Junction, Florida 34972
www.desertinnrestaurant.com
(407) 436-1054

Egmont Key
Egmont Key Alliance
P.O. Box 66238
St. Petersburg, FL 33736
www.egmontkey.org

Egmont Key State Park
(727) 893-2627
www.floridastateparks.org/egmontkey
www.hubbardsmarina.com/um/egmont.html

Anna Maria and Holmes Beach
Beach Bistro Restaurant
6600 Gulf Drive
Holmes Beach, Florida 34217
(941) 778-6444
www.beachbistro.com

Duffy's Tavern
5808 Marina Drive
Holmes Beach, Florida 34217
(941) 778-2501
www.duffystavernami.com

Harrington House Bed & Breakfast
5626 Gulf Drive
Holmes Beach, Florida 34217

(941) 778-5444
(888) 828-5566
www.harringtonhouse.com

Rod & Reel Pier Restaurant
875 North Shore Drive
Anna Maria, Florida 34216
(941) 778-1885

Sandbar Restaurant
100 Spring Avenue
Anna Maria, Florida 34216
(941) 778-0444
www.sandbar.groupersandwich.com

Cortez
Annie's Bait and Tackle
4334 127th Street West
Cortez, Florida 34215
(941) 794-3580
www.anniesbaitandtackle.com

Florida Maritime Museum
4415 119th Street West
Cortez, Florida 34215
(941) 708-6120
www.manateeclerk.com/historical/
MaritimeMuseum

N. E. Taylor Boatworks
12304 46th Avenue West
Cortez, Florida 34215
(941) 794-2582

Sea Hagg
12304 Cortez Road West
Cortez, Florida 34215
(941) 795-5756
www.seahagg.com

Star Fish Company Market and Dockside
Restaurant
12306 46th Avenue West
Cortez, Florida 34215
(941) 794-1243
www.starfishcompany.com

Lake Placid
Caladium Arts and Crafts Co-op
132 East Interlake Boulevard
Lake Placid, Florida 33852
(863) 699-5940
www.caladiumarts.org

Lake Placid Mural Society
18 North Oak Street
Lake Placid, Florida 33852
(863) 465-2394

Toby The Clown Foundation
Toby's Clown School
109 West Interlake Boulevard
Lake Placid, Florida 33852
(863) 465-2920
www.tobysclownfoundation.org

Arcadia
Arcadia All-Florida Championship Rodeo
124 Heard Street
Arcadia, Florida 34266
(863) 993-4343
www.arcadiarodeo.com

Heard Opera House Museum
106 West Oak Street
Arcadia, Florida 34266
(863) 494-9444
www.arcadiaoperahouse.com

Last Chapter Bookstore and Coffee
House
15 West Oak Street
Arcadia, Florida 34266
(863) 494-0506

Wheeler's Goody Café
13 South Monroe Avenue
Arcadia, Florida 34266
(863) 993-1555

South Region

Boca Grande
Anchor Inn
450 Fourth Street East
Boca Grande, Florida 33921
(800) 741-3074
www.anchorinnbocagrande.com

Boca Grande Fishing Guides Association
PO Box 676
Boca Grande, Florida 33921
(800) 667-1612
www.bocagrandefishing.com

Boca Grande Outfitters
375 Park Avenue
Boca Grande, Florida 33921
(941) 964-2445
www.bocagrandeoutfitters.com

Eagle Grille/ Boca Grande Marina
220 Harbor Drive
Boca Grande, Florida 33921
Restaurant: (941) 964-8000
www.eaglegrille.com
Marina: (941) 964-2100
www.bocagrandemarina.net

Fugate's
4th Street and Park Avenue
Boca Grande, Florida 33921
(941) 964-2323

Gasparilla Inn & Club
500 Palm Avenue
Boca Grande, Florida 33921
(941) 964-4500
(877) 403-0599
www.the-gasparilla-inn.com

Historic Boca Grande Lighthouse and
Museum
880 Belcher Road
Boca Grande, Florida 33921
(941) 964-0375
www.floridastateparks.org/gasparillaisland

Island Bike and Beach
333 Park Avenue
Boca Grande, Florida 33921
(941) 964-0711
www.islandbikeandbeach.com

Loose Caboose
Historic Depot Building
443 West Fourth Street
Boca Grande, Florida 33921
(941) 964-0440
www.loosecaboose.biz

Pink Elephant
491 Bayou Avenue
Boca Grande, Florida 33921
(941) 964-4540
www.the-gasparilla-inn.com/din_
pinkelephant.php

PJ's Seagrille
321 Park Avenue
Boca Grande, Florida 33921
(941) 964-0806
www.pjseagrille.com

Temptation Restaurant
350 Park Avenue
Boca Grande, Florida 33921
(941) 964-2610
www.temptationbocagrande.com

Whidden's Marina and Gasparilla Island
Maritime Museum
190 1st Street East
Boca Grande, Florida 33921
(941) 964-2878
Museum: (941) 964-4466
www.whiddensmarina.com

Clewiston
Clewiston Inn
108 Royal Palm Avenue
Clewiston, Florida 33440
(863) 983-8151
(800) 749-4466
www.clewistoninn.com

Briny Breezes
Town of Briny Breezes
4802 North Ocean Boulevard
Briny Breezes, Florida 33435
(561) 272-5495
www.townofbrinybreezes-fl.com

**Matlacha, Bokeelia, Pineland, and St.
James City**
Bert's Bar & Grill
4271 Pine Island Road
Matlacha, Florida 33993
(239) 282-3232
www.bertsbar.us

Bridgewater Inn
4331 Pine Island Road
Matlacha, Florida 33993
(239) 283-2423
(800) 378-7666
www.bridgewaterinn.com

Capt'n Con's Fish House
8421 Main Street
Bokeelia, Florida 33922
(239) 283-4300

Crossed Palms Gallery
8315 Main Street
Bokeelia, Florida 33922
(239) 283-2283

Elena's Jewelry
4606 Pine Island Road
Matlacha, Florida 33993
(239) 283-9658

Lovegrove Gallery
4637 Pine Island Road
Matlacha, Florida 33993
(239) 282-1244
www.leomalovegrove.com

Matlacha Island Cottages
4760 Pine Island Road
Matlacha, Florida 33993
(800) 877-7256
(239) 283-7368
www.islandcottages.com

Museum of the Islands
5728 Sesame Drive
Pine Island Center, Florida 33956
(941) 283-1525
www.museumoftheislands.com

Perfect Cup
4548 Pine Island Road
Matlacha, Florida 33993
(239) 283-4447

Tarpon Lodge
13771 Waterfront Drive
Pineland, Florida 33945
(239) 283-3999
www.tarponlodge.com

Waterfront Restaurant and Marina
2131 Oleander Street
St. James City, Florida 33956
(239) 283-0592
www.waterfrontrestaurant.com

Wild Child Art Gallery
4625 Pine Island Road
Matlacha, Florida 33993
(239) 283-6006
www.wildchildartgallery.com

Sanibel and Captiva
Bailey-Matthews Shell Museum
3075 Sanibel-Captiva Road
Sanibel, Florida 33957
(239) 395-2233
www.shellmuseum.org

Bubble Room
15001 Captiva Drive
Captiva Island, Florida 33924
(239) 472-5558
www.bubbleroomrestaurant.com

Captiva Chapel By The Sea
11580 Chapin Street
Captiva Island, Florida 33924
 (239) 472-1646
www.captivacivicassociation.com/html/
chapel_by-the-sea.html

Captiva Island Store
Corner of Andy Rosse Lane and Captiva
Drive
Captiva Island, Florida 33924
(239) 472-2374
www.captivaislandstore.com

The Castaways Beach Cottages
6460 Sanibel-Captiva Road
Sanibel Island, Florida 33957
(239) 472-1252
(800) 375-0152
www.castawayssanibel.com

Doc Ford's Sanibel Rum Bar & Grill
975 Rabbit Road
Sanibel Island, Florida 33957
(239) 472-8311
www.docfordssanibel.com

J. N. "Ding" Darling National Wildlife
Refuge
1 Wildlife Drive
Sanibel Island, Florida 33957
(239) 472-1100
www.fws.gov/dingdarling

Jungle Drums Gallery
11532 Andy Rosse Lane
Captiva Island, Florida 33924
(239) 395-2266
www.jungledrumsgallery.com

Mad Hatter Restaurant
6467 Sanibel-Captiva Road
Sanibel Island, Florida 33957
(239) 472-0033
www.madhatterrestaurant.com

Mucky Duck Restaurant
11546 Andy Rosse Lane
Captiva Island, Florida 33924
(239) 472-3434
www.muckyduck.com

Sanibel Bean
2240 Periwinkle Way
Sanibel Island, Florida 33957

(239) 395-1919
www.sanibelbean.com

South Seas Island Resort
5400 Plantation Road
Captiva Island, Florida 33924
(239) 472-5111
(866) 565-5089
www.southseas.com

Sunshine Seafood Café
14900 Captiva Drive
Captiva Island, Florida 33924
(239) 472-6200
www.sunshineseafoodftmyers.com/
About_Us.html

'Tween Waters Inn
15951 Captiva Drive
Captiva Island, Florida 33924
(239) 472-5161
(800) 223-5865
www.tween-waters.com

Twilight Café
2430 Periwinkle Way
Sanibel Island, Florida 33957
(239) 472-8818
www.twilightcafesanibel.com

Koreshan State Historic Site
Koreshan State Historic Site
3800 Corkscrew Road
Estero, Florida 33928
(239) 992-0311
www.floridastateparks.org/Koreshan

Goodland
Little Bar Restaurant
205 Harbor Place
Goodland, Florida 34140
(239) 394-5663
www.littlebarrestaurant.com

Old Marco Lodge Crab House
401 Papaya Street
Goodland, Florida 34140
(239) 642-7227
www.oldmarcolodge.com

Stan's Idle Hour Seafood Restaurant
221 Goodland Drive West
Goodland, Florida 34140
(239) 394-3041
www.stansidlehour.net

Everglades City, Chokoloskee Island, and Ochopee
Captain Doug's Airboat Tours
State Road 29
Everglades City, Florida 33929
(800) 282-9194
www.captaindougs.com

Everglades National Park
Gulf Coast Visitor Center
815 Oyster Bar Lane
Everglades City, Florida 34139
(239) 695-3311
www.nps.gov/ever/index.htm

Havana Café
191 County Road 29/Smallwood Drive
Chokoloskee, Florida 34138
(239) 695-2214
http://myhavanacafe.com/

Historic Ted Smallwood's Store
360 Mamie Street
P.O. Box 367
Chokoloskee, Florida 34138
(239) 695-2989

Ivey House Bed & Breakfast
107 Camellia Street
Everglades City, Florida 34139
(239) 695-3299
(877) 567-0679
www.iveyhouse.com

Joanie's Blue Crab Café
39395 Highway 41/Tamiami Trail
Ochopee, Florida 34141
(239) 695-2682

Museum of the Everglades
105 West Broadway
Everglades City, Florida 34139
(239) 695-0008
www.evergladesmuseum.org

Ochopee Post Office
38000 Highway 41/Tamiami Trail
Ochopee, Florida 34141
Rod and Gun Club
200 Broadway Street
Everglades City, Florida 34139
(239) 695-2100
www.evergladesrodandgun.com

Speedy Johnson's Airboat Rides
61 Begonia Street
Everglades City, Florida 33929
(239) 695-4448
www.speedyjohnsons.com/homed.htm

Card Sound
Alabama Jack's
58000 Card Sound Road
Card Sound, Florida 33037
(305) 248-8741
www.alabamajacks.com

Stiltsville
Located in Biscayne National Park
www.stiltsville.org

Tavernier and Islamorada
1935 Hurricane Monument
Mile Marker 81.8
Islamorada, Florida 33036

Cheeca Lodge & Spa
81801 Overseas Highway
Mile Marker 82
Islamorada, Florida 33036
(305) 664-4651
(800) 327-2888
www.cheeca.com

Green Turtle Inn
81219 Overseas Highway
Mile Marker 81.2

Islamorada, Florida 33036
(305) 664-2006
www.greenturtleinn.com

Tavernier Hotel
Mile marker 91.8
91865 Overseas Highway
Tavernier, Florida 33070
(305) 853-5015
www.tavernierhotel.com

Big Pine Key
Bahia Honda State Park
36850 Overseas Highway
Mile Marker 37
Big Pine Key, Florida 33043
(305) 872-3210
www.bahiahondapark.com

Barnacle Bed & Breakfast
1557 Long Beach Drive
Big Pine Key, Florida 33043
(305) 872-3298
(800) 465-9100
www.thebarnacle.net

National Key Deer Refuge Headquarters
28950 Watson Boulevard
Big Pine Key, Florida 33043
(305) 872-2239
www.fws.gov/nationalkeydeer

No Name Pub
30813 North Watson Boulevard
Big Pine Key, Florida 33043
(305) 872-9115
www.nonamepub.com

INDEX

Here are some other books from Pineapple Press on related topics. For a complete catalog, visit our website at www.pineapplepress.com. Or write to Pineapple Press, P.O. Box 3889, Sarasota, Florida 34230-3889, or call (800) 746-3275.

Florida's Finest Inns and Bed & Breakfasts, Second Edition, by Bruce Hunt. From warm and cozy bed & breakfasts to elegant and historic hotels, this is the definitive guide to Florida's most quaint, romantic, and often eclectic lodgings. With photos and charming pen-and-ink drawings by the author. (pb)

Best Backroads of Florida, Volumes 1, 2, and 3, by Douglas Waitley. Each volume in this series offers several well-planned day trips through some of Florida's least-known towns and well-traveled byways. You will glimpse a gentler Florida and learn lots about its history. Volume 1: The Heartland (Central Florida); Volume 2: Coasts, Glades, and Groves (South Florida); Volume 3: Beaches and Hills (North Florida). (pb)

Easygoing Guide to Natural Florida by Douglas Waitley. If you love nature but want to enjoy it with minimum effort, this is the series for you. Volume 1: South Florida; Volume 2: Central Florida. (pb)

Florida History from the Highways by Douglas Waitley. Journey along Florida's highways–I-75, US 41, I-95, US 27, US 98, and the Turnpike–learning all the roadside history along the way. Begins with a brief history of Florida. (pb)

Time Traveler's Guide to Florida by Jack Powell. A unique guidebook that offers more than 140 places and reenactments in Florida where you can experience the past, and a few where you can time travel into the future. (pb)

Historical Traveler's Guide to Florida, Second Edition, by Eliot Kleinberg. Visit Henry Plant's Tampa hotel, the wreck of the *San Pedro,* and Ernest Hemingway's Key West home. Here are 57 travel destinations in Florida of historical significance. (pb)

St. Augustine and St. Johns County: A Historical Guide by William R. Adams. A guide to the places and buildings where history can be found in America's oldest permanent settlement. Color photographs featured throughout. (pb)

Historic Homes of Florida, Second Edition, by Laura Stewart and Susanne Hupp. 68 notable dwellings open to the public, from humble Cracker houses to stately mansions. This new edition is updated and illustrated throughout with color photographs. (pb)

Florida's Museums and Cultural Attractions, Second Edition, by Doris Bardon and Murray D. Laurie. This newly updated guide has a destination to suit every interest. You'll find over 350 museums and attractions to choose from. (pb)